It's a Girl's Game Too

It's a Girl's Game Too

by Alice Siegel & Margo McLoone
designed & illustrated by Lisa Campbell Ernst

Holt, Rinehart and Winston/New York

To my sisters, Mary Kaye,
Annie and Patricia.
M. McL-B

For my mother, Ruth,
and George, Andrew, Howard, and Jimmy.
A. S.

Printed in the United States of America.
Designed by Lisa Campbell Ernst.

10 9 8 7 6 5 4 3 2

Library of Congress Cataloging in Publication Data

McLoone, Margo.
It's a girl's game too.

Includes index.
1. Sports for women.   I. Siegel, Alice, joint
author.   II. Ernst, Lisa Campbell.   III. Title.
GV709.M32   796'.0194   79-9422
ISBN 0-03-046526-5

ISBN 0-03-046526-5

It's a Girl's Game Too

Introduction 6

Chapter 1—The Way It Was 7
(A brief history of women and sports)

Chapter 2—Every Girl Can and Should Play 10

Chapter 3—How to Keep in Shape for Your Sport 17

Chapter 4—Team Sports 22

Baseball 23
Basketball 29
Ice Hockey 35
Field Hockey 41
Football 46
Lacrosse 52
Soccer 58
Softball 63
Volleyball 68

Chapter 5—Individual Sports 73

Bicycle Road Racing 74
Bowling 79
Distance Running 84
Golf 89
Racket Sports
(Tennis) 95
(Platform Tennis) 101
(Table Tennis) 105
Speed Ice-Skating 110
Speed Roller-Skating 115

Chapter 6—Sports Camps: How to Choose One 119

Chapter 7—How to Be in the Game Without Playing 121

Sports Associations for Instruction and Information 124

Glossary 125

Index 126

Introduction

Our research for this book has taken us around the country where we have watched young girls practice, play, and compete in a variety of sports. We have spoken with lots of people—the young athletes themselves, and their parents and coaches. Many of them felt that a book of this kind was long overdue. **It's a Girl's Game Too** was written to inspire and excite girls about the fun of sports as well as the physical and emotional benefits of playing. The intention of the book is to help girls get started in sports by familiarizing them with the basics of the games, so that they can select the sport that holds the most appeal for them or that they feel best suited for.

The history of each sport is given along with the rules of the game, game talk, how and where to play, and equipment needed.

Eighteen sports are covered. Among them: basketball and field hockey which girls have always played; football and ice hockey which were once closed to girls; and such all-time favorites as bowling and golf. In selecting racket sports, we chose tennis, the most familiar one; platform tennis, one of the newest ones; and table tennis, an internationally competitive sport. The four racing sports are cycling, roller skating, running, and ice skating. The result of this selection is a kaleidoscope of sports for young girls to play and enjoy.

CHAPTER 1
The Way It Was

When the Olympic games were held in ancient Greece in 776 B.C., women were forbidden to take part in the competition. In fact, if a woman was so much as caught watching the games, she was condemned and thrown to her death from Mount Typaion in Olympia. As a result, the women organized their own athletic events, which they called the Heraea in honor of the goddess Hera, queen of the Olympian gods. When the Romans conquered Greece they put a stop to these games, and that ended women's competition for two thousand years.

In 1919 a crusader for women's sports, Ethelda Bleibtrey, was arrested in New York City for taking off her stockings before going for a swim. Believe it or not, at that time it was against the law for a woman to expose her legs on a public beach. This was Ethelda's way of calling attention to the need to change the bathing costumes women were required to wear—bloomers and a dress, which not only prevented women from swimming but kept alive the myth that they were too weak and would drown if they tried. Ethelda Bleibtrey later went on to win America's first gold medal in freestyle swimming.

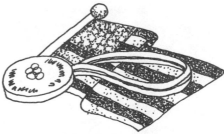

These are examples of how women have had to struggle to take part in sports. Women were not only kept down in sports, they were encouraged to stay in the safety of the home. It was understood that a woman was better suited to the use of a needle than to exercise.

Dressed in clothing that covered her body from top to toe, she was kept away from any activity that brought color to her cheeks—something to be avoided by all respectable women.

Gradually there were changes. At first women were allowed to play archery and croquet. These were recreational games played with men as part of the social life of the times. Then the bicycle was invented and cycling became a very popular sport. The long dresses of the day made it difficult and dangerous for women to ride, but they could not be kept off the bicycle. A divided skirt was created for them, to make cycling safe. Bicycle fashion soon became street fashion, and a new look for women was on its way. Changes in clothing gave women a freedom of movement they had never known. They abandoned the heavy bathing dresses for comfortable swimming suits. They put on pants so that they could ride astride a horse instead of side-saddle.

By the 1920s women were playing a variety of sports such as golf, tennis, and basketball. However, female athletes were the exception rather than the rule, and there were many games they weren't

Jock Semple, official, moving in to intercept Ms. Switzer, then being bounced himself.

allowed to play.

In 1967 a woman registered as K. Switzer to run in the all-male Boston Marathon. During the race, an official discovered she was a woman and tried to pull her out of the race. The publicity that resulted from that incident forced a change in the rules. In 1972, five years later, women were permitted to enter marathons. In that same year, the federal government passed a law, Title IX, that promised to give girls and women equal opportunities in sports.

At last, in the late 1970s, the time arrived when girls could step out onto the playing fields and play any sport they chose. Women have struggled to get where they are today and are finally in a position to enjoy the freedom they worked for.

CHAPTER 2
Every Girl Can and Should Play

Times have changed. Not only are sports more available to girls today, but our modern way of life demands exercise for healthier living. Taking part in sports is a fun way of keeping fit. Everybody knows that. Yet, many girls don't play. Why not? One reason may be that many of them still believe things about girls in sports that are no longer true. Let's do away with some of the myths that may have kept you and other girls off the playing fields.

Sports Make Girls Unfeminine

Sports do not make girls unfeminine. The firm bodies and glow of health that girls get from athletic activity make them more attractive. There is beauty in seeing a female athlete using her body with precision, displaying grace and strength.

Female Athletes Are Born, Not Made

It is true that learning the skills of a game is easier for some girls than for others, just as it is easier for some boys than others. But there is no such thing as a born athlete.

Every athlete has to practice to become good. An example of great athletic determination is Wilma Rudolph. She spent the first six years of her life with a crippled leg and later went on to win three Olympic gold medals in track and field.

Girls Who Are Athletic Build Ugly Muscles

This is not so. Girls and boys are built differently. When girls exercise, their bodies become firm and well toned, not big and bulky. Tennis player Chris Evert and ice skater Dorothy Hamill are good examples of female athletes with strong, sleek bodies.

Girls Will Get Hurt If They Participate in Sports

A normally healthy girl has no reason to be afraid of injury. If you stay in shape, know the sport you're playing, and wear the proper equipment, your chances of being injured are no greater than a boy's.

Girls Shouldn't Be Active When They Are Menstruating

This is ridiculous! Women have won Olympic medals during their menstrual period. Doctors now believe that not only can girls participate in strenuous exercise at any time, but doing so can lessen pain and discomfort.

Girls Shouldn't Play Boys' Sports

There is no such thing as separate sports for boys and girls. This is a myth that is taking a long time to die. Today, girls are trying and succeeding at every sport. This includes ice hockey and football, which were once thought of as sports for boys and men only.

Boys Should Be Coached by Men— Girls Should Be Coached by Women

It doesn't matter if your coach is a man or a woman. What is important is that you have a good coach who knows the sport and is willing to help you. Today there are women coaching male athletes as well as men who coach women's teams.

Girls Are Not Interested in Sports

This may seem to be the case because girls have not played in as great numbers as boys have. But for years girls have been discouraged and discriminated against in sports. Given a chance to play, they show the same enthusiasm for sports as boys.

Girls Can't Play As Well As Boys So They Shouldn't Try

A comparison between boys and girls is unfair because boys have been encouraged and trained to be athletic for a long time and girls haven't. Actually there are more differences between players of the same sex than there are between boys and girls. Remember, the fun of sports is in the playing. You will find that the greatest satisfaction comes from improving your own game and playing your best.

Now that you know some of the reasons why girls haven't played, let's look at some good reasons why they should play.

Sports Can Help You . . .

Stay Healthy. Physical activity strengthens your whole body including your heart, lungs, and muscles. A strong body is better able to fight illness.

Become Strong. Females have always been considered the weaker sex. They have had to rely on men to do everything for them from opening jars to carrying suitcases. Sports activities will make you stronger and more self-reliant.

Become More Graceful. You can develop the same grace and poise from sports as you would from dancing lessons. Consider the beauty of movement of the gymnast on the balance beam and the skater gliding across the ice.

Fight Fat. As you grow older the percentage of your body fat increases. You are more likely to put on extra weight from being inactive

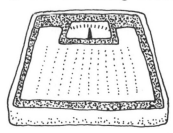

than from overeating. Exercise turns baby fat to muscle and if continued on a regular basis, it can keep you trim and firm.

Improve Your Posture Without Trying. Athletes don't have to be told to stand up tall, they do it naturally! When your muscles are firm they support your body better. They get this way from exercise.

Sleep Better. If you can't sleep at night, maybe you didn't move around enough during the day. You'll sleep better after exercising than you will after watching TV.

Take Good Care of Yourself. As an athlete, you'll want to eat right and get enough rest so that you can play better.

When You Are Feeling Angry. When you feel angry and frustrated, you can do something about it. Put on your sneakers and go for a run or grab a basketball and shoot a few baskets and see the angry feelings disappear.

Overcome Shyness. Playing sports puts you in contact with new people and different situations. Many athletes believe that if it weren't for sports, they would still be shy and afraid of people.

Learn to Take Criticism. It takes time to learn a sport. You will make mistakes as you learn. Listening to criticism from your coach and teammates will help you improve your skills.

When You Are Feeling Blue. It's hard to feel sad when you are riding a bike or out on a run. Doctors often prescribe exercise for depression.

Learn How to Lose. No one likes to lose, but it's part of playing the game. You can't win all the time, and thinking about why you lost and what you can do to improve is sometimes more important than winning.

Learn to Control Your Temper. Children as well as adults who don't control their tempers on the playing fields don't belong there. When things get hot you should learn to stay cool. Controlling emotions is an important part of sportsmanship.

Learn How to Get Along with Others. Sports won't teach you to like everyone, but they will help you learn to play with people. This is especially true in team sports, where everyone must play together in order to win.

Overcome Fear. There are lots of things in life to be afraid of. But when you learn how to catch a fast ball coming toward you—a fast ball that once frightened you—you are learning how to fight fear.

Learn How to Win. Whatever your sport may be, you are a winner when you achieve the goals you have set for yourself. And remember, a true winner is always kind and gracious to her opponent.

See the Good in You. When you give your best effort, you should be proud of yourself. Take notice of all the good things you do in practice and in play and tell yourself you're doing fine.

Do Better School Work. When you tune up your body, your brain works better. One junior high school found that after putting failing students into a physical fitness program, their grades and behavior improved.

Learn to Play by the Rules. When an official like an umpire makes a call you may not agree with, you must accept the ruling. Rules are rules, and you have to learn to live with them.

Learn to Make Quick Decisions. Once you are out on the playing field you learn to react quickly. Your coach can't tell you how to handle every play. You have to make the decision. Sometimes you'll be right, sometimes you'll be wrong. At least you will have made a decision and you can learn from your mistakes.

Learn How to Be Competitive. When you participate in sports you train your body and mind to compete. Learning how to compete to win a game will help you to compete for the things you want in life.

Find a Career You Never Thought About. If you are hooked on sports you may discover a new career. Today there are new opportunities for women in the world of sports. The more you know about sports, the better qualified you'll be for these jobs.

Things to Think About When Choosing a Sport

There is a great variety of sports, and it should be easy to find one or more that you will enjoy playing. Start with a sport that will be easy and fun for you. Ask yourself these questions before selecting a sport.

Jean Champion

Members of St. Joseph's School for the Deaf Track Club after the finish of a 6.2 mile race.

Every Girl Can and Should Play. Sports do not exclude the handicapped. There are blind golfers, wheelchair tournaments in table tennis, and bowling for the physically handicapped to name a few of the possibilities.

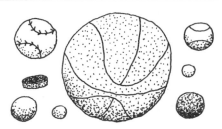

Is there a place nearby for me to play the sport? This is important. There is no point in choosing a sport that doesn't exist in your community or is hard to get to. Investigate the area you live in to find out what sport facilities are available. Start by looking in the yellow pages or classified section of your phone book.

What's best for me, individual or team sports? You have to know yourself to answer this question. Individual sports are played alone or with a partner. If you need a partner, be sure you have a friend who will enjoy playing too. Individual sports are best for people who like to set their own pace and have the self-discipline to practice by themselves. Team sports are for those who prefer playing with a group. Find out about teams in your area. A point to remember: Being part of a team means you must be available to practice when they do.

Will I need lessons? In order to learn some sports you need formal instruction. Find out what lessons are offered free by the local parks and recreation department. Private instructors can easily be found at local sports clubs, but that costs money.

How expensive will the sport be? Be sure you can afford the sport you choose. Equipment costs are different for each sport. If expensive equipment is necessary, you may want to rent or borrow it while you are trying the sport. If you need lessons, find out the total cost. Ask if there will be additional charges for things like the use of a court or rink.

Try to learn at least one sport that can be played and enjoyed throughout your lifetime. Some of the sports that are considered lifetime sports are: skating, golf, racket sports, cycling, bowling, and running. For each sport discussed in this book we have supplied the name and address at the end of the book for an organization that promotes and encourages participation in that sport. By writing to these various organizations, you can find out information that can be valuable to you when selecting a sport.

Follow These Pointers When You Are Learning Your Sport

- When you learn a new sport you may feel less self-conscious if you practice skills when you are alone or with a good friend.
- Once you are comfortable playing with others, don't hesitate to play with players who are better. It is a good way for you to improve your game.
- You can make the most of your practice by imagining that you are in a game situation at all times.
- Keep your eyes and ears open for clinics and free demonstrations being offered on your sport.
- Learn how the game is played by watching others. Professional and Olympic sports events are televised, but exciting amateur play can be found in your own town or city.
- Keep this in mind. The more you play the better you will play, and the better you play any sport, the more exciting and rewarding it will be for you.
- Don't try to learn the whole game at once. Learn one skill at a time. Have a purpose, and set a goal for each practice period.
- Don't compare yourself with other people—compare yourself to you and whether and how much you improve each day.

CHAPTER 3
How to Keep in Shape for Your Sport

As an athlete, you will use your body in new and exciting ways. Knowing how to take good care of yourself will make you feel better and perform better. Here are some Do's and Don'ts to help.

• Don't eat just before you play. Your body needs time to adjust from digestion to exercise.

• Do keep in shape for your sport by staying active. Jumping rope for 3 to 5 minutes a day is a convenient and vigorous exercise. When you have a choice, climb the stairs rather than take an elevator. Instead of waiting for a bus or car ride, try walking or jogging to the places you have to go.

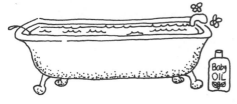

• Do use lukewarm water for your baths. Add a little baby oil to the water for extra moisture.

• Do keep your hair covered when you are outdoors in the winter. Freezing temperatures can damage your hair.

• Do keep your hair out of your eyes by wearing braids, clips, elastic-coated rubber bands, or a sweatband when you play.

• Do prevent eyeglasses from clouding over on hot humid days by dipping the lenses in cold water before playing or racing. Wipe them off thoroughly with a handkerchief.

• Do put petroleum jelly (Vaseline) or lip gloss on your lips to avoid chapped lips in cold weather.

• Don't wear jewelry, especially rings, during practice or a game. They can cause serious injury to you or to other players.

• Don't eat or drink dairy products, which take a long time to digest, before practice or a game.

• Do chew ice and drink cold beverages to give you quick refreshment. They will not cause cramps and will refresh you faster than lukewarm liquids.

• Do drink plenty of water during the day. It is very good for you. One way to get into the habit of drinking water is to keep a bottle of cold water in the refrigerator. If you don't like the taste of water where you live, boil it for five minutes first and let it cool, then pour it into a bottle and refrigerate it. It should taste better.

• Don't drink sodas and drinks with sugar in them. Natural fruit juices are much better for you and they taste good too.

• Do eat fresh fruits, vegetables, and whole grain products like bran muffins and whole wheat bread. An oatmeal cookie will give you energy that will last much longer than a soda or candy bar.

• Do eat foods that are rich in iron, such as molasses, apricots, raisins, whole grain breads, eggs, leafy green vegetables, chicken, and liver.

• Do eat foods that are made with honey or are naturally sweet (fruit) when you crave something sweet.

• Do start your day with breakfast. If you think you don't like to eat breakfast, maybe you should change what you eat. If that doesn't work, try a nourishing breakfast drink.

Here are some food ideas for a healthier, happier you.

Breakfast Ideas

• Peanut butter on graham crackers or whole wheat toast.

• Open-face grilled cheese on whole wheat bread.
• Whole wheat pancakes with honey.
• Plain yoghurt with honey and toasted wheat germ.
• Banana milk shake. (Put a banana, a cup of milk, a raw egg, and a teaspoon of honey into the blender and blend. Don't worry about the egg; you won't be able to taste it.)

Snack and Dessert Ideas

• Mix together equal parts of shelled nuts, raisins, and sunflower seeds. Pour the mixture into small plastic bags and tie. This makes a convenient snack that you can carry anywhere.

• Peel a ripe banana and roll it first in honey, then in finely ground nuts. Insert a stick at the bottom of the banana (for easy handling) and put it in the freezer for at least one hour.

• Spread out pineapple chunks (the kind that come in their own natural juice) on a tray and freeze for one hour or more so they remain in individual pieces. Take the frozen chunks and divide them into small snack-size plastic bags. Tie the bags and put back into the freezer. They make handy snack packs for hot days.

• Make your own fruitsicles: Pour fruit juice into any ice tray and freeze.

• Make peanut popcorn: Mix six cups of freshly popped corn and one cup of peanuts. Melt 1/4 cup butter and tablespoon of peanut butter and toss over mixture.

• Add a dollop of fresh whipped cream to slices of apple, orange, and banana.

Drinks

• Make an orange soda: Add 2 tablespoons of frozen orange juice concentrate to one glass of club soda.

• Make a fruit punch: Combine pineapple juice, straw-berries, and honey in a blender.

• Make a fruit milk shake: Blend 1/2 cup of fresh berries, a teaspoon of honey, a teaspoon of lemon juice, and a cup of milk in a blender.

Coping with Minor Injuries

Even professional athletes get minor ailments. After all, that is how athlete's foot got its name. In many cases you can avoid problems by preventing them. Here are some suggestions.

Athlete's Foot. This is the itchiness and peeling between toes that is caused by a fungus which is often picked up in locker rooms. It can be avoided by wearing something on your feet in the dressing rooms and public showers. Dusting your feet with medicated powder is also helpful. Change your socks daily.

Blisters. They can be prevented by wearing proper-fitting shoes. Some athletes avoid getting blisters by putting petroleum jelly between

19

toes and all over their feet. If you do get blisters (you can get them on your hands too) it's best to leave them unbroken. Never peel off the skin if the blister pops. Apply tape over the blister and just leave it alone until the skin heals.

Bloody Nose. Keep your head in a normal upright position and apply pressure by pinching your nostrils together.

Bumps and Bruises. To keep swelling down and soothe the pain, apply a cold compress. An ice cube will do.

Eyes. Do not rub eyes that have been irritated by wind or dust. Instead, flush the eye with water. Normally this is done with an eyecup. If one is not available, cup your hand, pour water into it, tilt your head back, and let the water flow over the irritated eye.

If you wear eyeglasses while playing, it's a good idea to wear an elastic band that wraps around the back of your head to keep the glasses from falling off.

Floor Burns. When skin is scraped by falling or sliding on a gym floor, treat it by cleaning thoroughly, then cover with sterile gauze.

Ingrown Nails. Avoid this by keeping your toenails well trimmed. Always cut straight across the toenail to prevent ingrown nails.

Side Stitch. This is a sharp pain in the side of the body near the rib cage that people sometimes get when running. A side stitch is a spasm of your breathing muscles (diaphragm) and can often be avoided by warming up the diaphragm with deep breaths before you run. If you do get a side stitch in the middle of a run, press your hand over the area of pain, slow down, relax, and it will pass.

Sunburn. You can protect your face from sunburn by wearing a sun visor. An added benefit of a sun visor is that it allows body heat to escape through the top of your head. Keep the rest of your body free from sunburn by wearing lotion. When you buy sun lotion, check to see that PABA, which is a sunscreen, is one of the ingredients.

Torn Nails. To avoid the discomfort and pain involved,

keep your nails well trimmed. If a nail tears, trim around it and tape it.

Wind Knocked Out. When you temporarily lose your breath from a blow, lie down and bring your knees up to your chest in a relaxed position.

Windburn. On cold and windy days, wear a moisturizing lotion and dab petroleum jelly around your eyes and on your lips to prevent chapping.

For additional information on first aid, write to: .

Cramer's Youth League
First Aid Handbook
Cramers Products Inc.
P. O. Box 1001
Gardner, Kansas 66030

CHAPTER 4
Team Sports

Baseball

Baseball is a great game for a beginner. The whole game is eye-hand coordination, and it gets you ready for any other sport.
Amy Dickinson. Pitcher, shortstop. One of the first girls to play Little League baseball. Three-time All-Star Little Leaguer.

Baseball, probably America's favorite sport, is considered the great American pastime. A game similar to it called "rounders" was brought to the United States by the English in the early 1880s. In that game upright stakes were placed at each base and a batter would run around the stakes. The opposing team threw the ball at him, trying to hit him

with it, in order to get him out. Later, the stakes were replaced by bags of sand, and the runners were tagged by the ball instead of being hit by it. These and other changes went into the making of the modern game of baseball.

There were a number of women's baseball teams in the 1880s. One, called the Black Stocking Nine, was even pictured on an early set of baseball cards. These teams were the exception. For the most part it has been very difficult for females to play on organized baseball teams. Since 1974, Little League teams have been accepting female players, and today there are many more opportunities for girls to play. The leagues are divided into two age groups: for eight- to twelve-year-olds and for thirteen- to fifteen-year-olds.

Where You Play

A regulation baseball field is called a diamond, because of the shape made by the placement of the bases.

A baseball field can be set up in any large area near your home, such as a field, vacant lot, or playground. The one

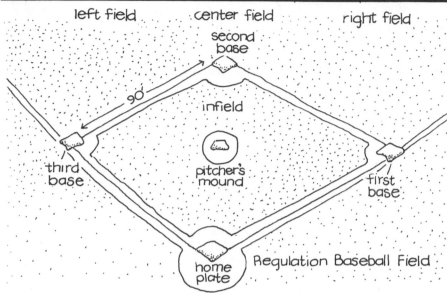

left field   center field   right field

second base

90'

infield

third base

pitcher's mound

first base

home plate

Regulation Baseball Field

thing to watch out for is that you are not too close to buildings with windows that can be broken or busy roads where the ball may roll into traffic.

Who the Players Are

There are two teams of nine players each. Only one team is in the field at a time. The team in the field is called the defense. The players are:

Pitcher. She throws the ball to the batter. She must also be able to field the ball and cover the bases. She should have a strong throwing arm.

Catcher. She stands behind the batter at home plate and catches the balls thrown by the pitcher. She must be able to stay in a squatting position for a long time.

Infield. First Baseman, Second Baseman, Shortstop, Third Baseman. They catch ground balls and short flies to the infield and cover the bases. Because they are close to the batter, they must have quick reflexes.

Outfield. Right Fielder, Center Fielder, Left Fielder. They catch the long balls. Those players need to be fast moving because they have to cover a large area.

Game Talk

Bases Loaded. This is a game situation when there are runners on first, second, and third base.

Base Stealing. To advance to a base by running for it when the opposing team is caught off guard.

Bunt. By holding the bat almost motionless, the batter gently hits the ball so that it rolls slowly along the ground.

Error. When a player in the field misplays a batted ball, allowing the hitter to reach base.

Grand Slam. A home run with the bases loaded.

Grounder. A batted ball that moves along the ground.

Hits. Single— when the batter gets one base on a hit. Double—when the batter gets two bases on a hit. Triple— when the batter gets three bases on a hit. **Home run**— when the batter hits a ball al-lowing her to go around all three bases and score.

Innings. The playing periods that divide the game. An inning is completed when each team has had a turn at bat. The top of the inning is when the first team is at bat; the bottom of the inning is when the second team is at bat.

Line Drive. A ball that has been hit hard and moves in a fairly straight line.

Pop Fly. A ball that is hit short and very high.

Relay. A ball thrown from the outfield to an infielder and then on to home plate or another base.

Sacrifice. A ball hit when

Jane Silver

Shortstop and fielder prepare to catch the ball.

there are less than two out, which allows another player to go to the next base or to score.

Southpaw. A left-handed pitcher.

Strike Zone. This is the area over home plate at which a ball must be pitched for it to be a strike (a good pitch). The strike zone is between the batter's knees and shoulders.

How the Game Is Played

Baseball is played by two teams. Each team takes turns playing offense (at bat) and defense (in the field). The team at bat stays there until they have made three outs. An out can be made in many ways. The most common ones are:

Strikeout. This is when the batter gets three strikes, either by swinging at and missing a pitched ball or by letting a ball pitched in the strike zone go by without swinging at it. The umpire signals that the ball was in the strike zone, and this is known as a "called strike."

Ground Out. This is when a hit ball bounces along the ground and is picked up by a fielder who throws it to the first baseman. If the first baseman touches the base before the batter reaches it, the batter is out.

Fly Out. This is when a ball hit by the batter is caught by a fielder before it touches the ground—the batter is out.

The team at bat scores a run every time one of its players goes from base to base and eventually reaches home plate. The batter can get on base by a walk, a hit, or an error. She can **walk** to first base if the pitcher has thrown four pitches that were outside of the strike zone. A **hit** is when the player has hit a good ball and can reach base before being tagged or before the ball reaches the fielder at that base.

Players move around the bases to home plate, depending on the number and type of hits the players at bat get.

When both teams have each had one turn at bat it is called an inning. There are nine innings in a game (seven for Little League). The team with the most runs scored at the end of the game wins.

Equipment and Clothing

Bat. A regulation Little League bat should not be longer than 33 inches. Bats are made of wood or metal and come in different weights. Try a bat before you buy it. It should be comfortable to hold and easy to swing.

Baseball. It is a hard ball, 3 inches in diameter, covered with white leather.

Gloves and Mitts. There are three different kinds. The catcher and first baseman's **mitts** have a sheath for the thumb only. The fielder's **glove** has separate sheaths for each finger and the thumb. When you are starting out choose a fielder's glove. It can be used for most positions.

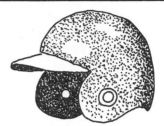
batting helmet

fielder's glove
baseball
←3"→
bat
rubber cleated shoe

Clothing. If you play for a team, you will probably wear a team uniform. If not, jeans or shorts with loose comfortable tops are best. A hat gives good protection from the sun. Batting helmets are usually supplied by the team. An all-purpose sneaker or rubber-cleated shoe is proper foot-wear.

What Makes a Good Player

Baseball is a game of running, hitting, throwing, and catching. You must be able to perform all of these skills. However, you can be much better at one than the others and still enjoy playing the game well.

Helpful Hints

If you have cleated shoes, clean them carefully after each use to make them last longer.

Always keep your glove in a safe, dry place. A good way to break in a new leather glove is to rub it with linseed oil or saddle soap, then put a baseball in the pocket of the glove. Close the glove around it. Tie it tightly with twine or string and keep it tied like this for a week.

It's a good idea to label your equipment. Write your name on the palm of your glove or the strap across the wrist and on a piece of adhesive tape on the nub of the bat.

When using a wooden bat, keep the trademark facing up. In this position a bat has the most punch. It also makes it less likely to crack.

At the end of the season, put all your equipment in an old pillowcase, or a receptacle like it. This will keep it all together and prevent it from getting lost.

To get the most out of your practices and games, warm up beforehand. You can do this by loosening up your arm with short, gentle throws, body stretches, and wind sprints. Wind sprints are a series of short runs at top speed.

Where to Write for More Information

If you write to the following, they will send you official regulations and playing rules for all age groups:

Little League Baseball

Little League Headquarters
P. O. Box 3485
Williamsport, Pennsylvania 17701

Western Region
6707 Little League Dr.
San Bernadino, California 92407

Southern Region
P. O. Box 13366
St. Petersburg, Florida 33733

Texas
1612 S. University Parks Dr.
Waco, Texas 76706

Central State Headquarters
Illinois Benedictine College
5700 College Rd.
Lisle, Illinois 60432

Canada
235 Dale Avenue
Ottawa, Ontario
Canada KI60H6

Babe Ruth Baseball
P. O. Box 5000
Trenton, New Jersey 08638

Pitch, hit, and run contests are held throughout the United States every spring. Information on how and where to participate is announced during the months of March and April on TV, radio, and in the newspapers.

Basketball

Playing basketball has given me a way to release my energy as well as a feeling of great pride for having worked hard to achieve something important for me.

Carol Blazejowski. One of America's foremost women's basketball players. Member of U.S. women's team.

In 1891 when Dr. James Naismith found his physical education students were bored with their regular exercise, he decided to do something about it. He hung two peach baskets from the gym balconies, gave the students a ball, and started them in a game of throwing the ball into the baskets. The game of basketball was born. Only one year later women were playing too. For years they played on business and church teams and later in schools. But it wasn't until recently that women's basketball was taken seriously. In 1976 it became an Olympic event, and in 1978 the first women's professional league was formed.

One of the great things about basketball is that it can be played almost anywhere, indoors and out. All you need is a basketball and a hoop. If you decide to play, you will find that it does great things for your overall health. It is a good sport for strengthening your upper body, an area where girls are often weak.

Where You Play

You can play and practice basketball anywhere you find a basket or hoop. They are everywhere: in city playgrounds, school yards, and hanging from garages, barns, and sheds.

A regulation basketball court has two baskets at each end.

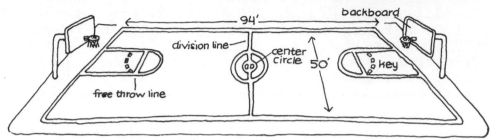

Regulation Basketball Court

Who the Players Are

Basketball is played by two teams. Because the same players on a team must quickly switch from offense to defense, each player must be able to shoot, pass, dribble, guard, and rebound. A team is made up of the following players:

Guards 2. They usually bring the ball up the court and get it to the teammates who are nearest the basket. They are often the better ball-handlers of the team, which means they are good at dribbling and passing.

Forwards 2. Their strength is scoring and rebounding, and they play in positions near the sides of the basket.

Center. Often the tallest player on the team, she plays in an area in front of the basket. Usually she takes part in the center jump ball that starts the game.

Game Talk

Basket. 1) The goal through which the ball must pass in order to score, known as the hoop. 2) A successful shot that is worth two points.

Dribble. To bounce the basketball with one hand while on the move.

Dunk. A shot made by leaping high in the air and jamming the ball through the basket.

Foul. When a player does something illegal to another player, like tripping or holding her, it is a **personal foul.** The player who was fouled against is allowed one or more free throws. When a rule of the game is violated—for example, delay of game, arguing with the referee or unsportsman-like conduct—it is a **technical foul.** A player from the other team is allowed one or more free throws.

Free Throw. A shot from behind the free throw line that is given to a player because of a foul by the opponents. Each free throw is worth one point.

Guarding. This is when the players try to keep their opponents from scoring by preventing them from receiving a passed ball or from getting in a good position to score.

Jump Ball. This is how the game is started and, in some cases, restarted after a stop in play: One player from each team stands opposite the other, the referee tosses the ball into the air above them, and they both jump and try to tip the ball to their own teammates.

Lay-up. A shot made by a player who drives toward the basket, jumps up, and bounces the ball against the backboard so that it drops down through the basket.

Dribbling the basketball.

One-on One. A game played by two players usually at one basket. One player plays defense, the other, offense. A player can keep the ball as long as she continues to score.

Pass. To throw the ball to a teammate.

Rebound. To get a ball that was thrown at the basket, but that bounced away instead of going in.

Shoot. To throw the ball toward the basket in an attempt to score.

Traveling. Walking or running with the ball without dribbling.

Turnover. When a team loses the ball and it is turned over to the other team.

Violation. When a player violates a rule of the game and the ball is turned over to the other team. Two common violations are: **double-dribble,** which is stopping the dribble and then beginning again, and **three second rule,** when a member of the offensive team (the one that has the ball) stands in the key for more than three seconds.

How the Game Is Played

Basketball is played by two teams of five players each. The object of the game is to score the most points by throwing the ball into the opponent's basket. Each successful throw

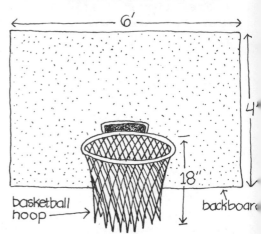

basketball hoop ⟶   ⟵ backboard

6'   4'   18"

is scored as two points except for that thrown from the free throw line after a foul, which counts as one. The players move the ball around the court by dribbling it or passing it to other players on their team. No one is allowed to walk or run with the ball held in their hands. Because basketball is a noncontact sport, the players may not shove, hold, tackle, or hit their opponents. They try to get the ball away from the other team by stealing it, intercepting passes, and rebounding.

Until a few years ago, women's basketball was played with six players instead of five. The rules of that game were quite different from those of the men's game. Some states, like Iowa, where girls' high school basketball draws more spectators than the boys' game, still play with six players. But the trend is toward five-woman basketball in which the rules, except for a few, are like those of men's basketball. One exception is the thirty-second-clock rule which says that a team must shoot the ball within thirty seconds after crossing the midcourt. In boys' high school basketball there is no such rule.

Equipment and Clothing

Ball and Hoop. A regulation-size basketball is not less than 29 1/2 inches in circumference and weighs from 20 to 22 ounces. In 1979 a new ball, 3 percent smaller in weight and circumference, was introduced to women's professional

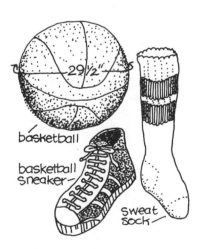

basketball

basketball sneaker

sweat sock

play. If you would like to put up your own hoop, you can buy one in a sporting goods store.

It should be mounted 10 feet above the ground on a backboard.

Clothing. Your footwear is the most important part of your outfit. Basketball sneakers should give good protection to your ankles. Sneakers which are made with a high cut on the upper part of the sole are best for this. Now that so many girls and women are playing basketball, special basketball sneakers are being designed for them. If you already have a pair of all-court sneakers, they will do fine. A good, thick pair of sweat socks should be worn to absorb moisture and cushion your feet. Be sure to wear a pair of sweat socks when trying on and buying sneakers.

If you play basketball with a school team, you will usually be wearing a uniform or gym suit. When you play indoors or play in the summer, shorts and a loose top will serve you well. If you play outdoors in the cold weather, sweat pants are suggested with layers of clothing on top so you can peel things off as you get warm.

What Makes a Good Player

Carol Blazejowski, one of America's best woman basketball players, says you don't have to be real tall to play basketball. Your head is more important than your height. Knowing how to handle yourself on the court is essential. A good basketball player must be able to shoot, pass, and dribble the ball. All of these skills must be learned and developed.

Helpful Hints

You have to learn how to dribble the ball with your fingers. Try this when you practice: Rub some flour on the palm of your hand. When you've finished dribbling, look to see how much flour is still on your palm. If it is completely gone, it means that you are not using your fingers.

To practice jumping, jump as high as you can and make a mark on a wall. Keep jumping to that point and then try jumping higher.

Make every practice count. Most coaches say that players will play like they practice. When you practice, imagine that the stands are filled with fans and everyone is watching you.

You can practice with a friend by playing one-on-one or matching baskets.

Good exercises for playing basketball are skipping rope and sprinting.

Where to Write for More Information

Learn the rules by writing to

Official Collegiate
Basketball Guide
College Athletic
Publishing Service
349 East Thomas Road
Phoenix, Arizona 85012

Learn about shooting contests for young people by writing to

Hot Shot Coordinator
Pepsi Cola Co.
Anderson Hill Road
Purchase, New York 19577

Find out about women's professional basketball by writing to

Women's Professional
Basketball League
5150 East Main Street
Columbus, Ohio 43213

Contact your local YWCA for information about team play.

Ice Hockey

Ice hockey has everything: it's a game of speed on skates, demanding skill and agility, and offering unlimited excitement!
Laura Stamm. Skating coach for the New York Islanders hockey team.

The game of ice hockey, known as the fastest team sport on earth, was first played in Canada in the late 1800s. No one knows exactly how the game started. Some historians say that it was first played by Canadian soldiers who, when they couldn't play field hockey in winter, adapted the game so it could be played on ice.

Americans were playing ice hockey by 1893. It was

most popular in the northern areas of the United States, where frozen lakes and ponds were numerous. After indoor ice rinks were built, the game quickly spread throughout the country. But it was only recently that girls and women began to play. Today more and more girls are playing ice hockey because it combines the fun of skating with the excitement of the game.

Ice hockey, a great fitness-building sport, is especially good for the legs and pelvis. It is also a sport that will help you learn how to think on your feet and be assertive.

Where You Play

If you live in an area that has skating surfaces in the winter, you can begin by playing there. (Set up two goals at the opposite ends of the ice.) You can buy inexpensive practice goal nets at sporting goods stores or simply drop old sweat shirts to mark the goal area.

Who the Players Are

There are six players on a team.

Forwards 3. These offensive players are also known as

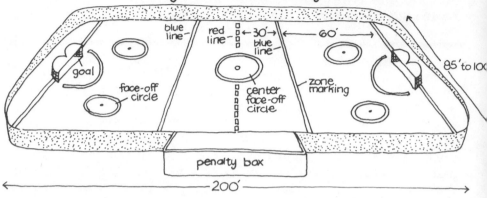

Regulation Ice Hockey Rink

blue line · red line · 30' · blue line · 60' · 85' to 100'

goal

face-off circle

zone marking

center face-off circle

penalty box

←——————— 200' ———————→

the **line.** They should be fast skaters and good shots, since their main job is scoring.

Defensive Players 2. Their main job is to help the goalie defend the goal. They try to break up plays and take the puck away from the other team.

Goalkeeper 1. Her job is to stop the puck from entering the goal. She can use her stick, glove, or body. She must have quick hands and excellent eyesight.

Hockey teams are divided into these age groups.

Tyke or Pony—ages 5-10
Pee Wee—ages 10-12
Bantam—ages 12-14

Game Talk

Deke. To fake or deliberately mislead an opponent.

Face-off. This is how the puck is put into play. Two opponents face each other with

their backs to their own goals. The referee drops the puck between the two players and they both try to get possession of it.

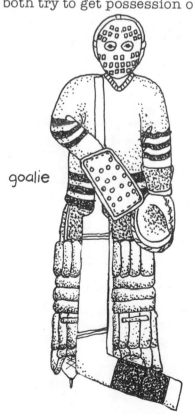

goalie

36

Feeding. Passing the puck from one player to the next.

Freezing. This is when the puck is pinned against the boards by a stick or skates and the play is stopped.

Icing. Shooting the puck the full length of the rink.

Offside. This occurs when a player skates over the blue line before the puck is moved across the blue line by a teammate.

Penalty Box. A separate bench where a player sits for a certain amount of time after a penalty.

How the Game Is Played

Ice hockey is played on ice between two teams who wear ice skates and carry sticks which they use to move a rubber disk called a puck. Players are not allowed to move the puck with their hands or any part of their body. The object of the game is to shoot the puck into the opponent's goal in order to score. Each goal is worth one point. The play is divided into three periods. Within the periods, the play is continuous except for fouls and timeouts. Players are substituted without a stop in the game.

In girls' hockey there is a "no checking" rule. This means that players are not allowed to hit or bump against other players in order to get the puck.

Holding or tripping opponents is never allowed. For

Margo McLoone-Basta

A face-off begins the play.

fouls such as these a player is made to sit in a penalty box. The team must continue to play without her until the penalty time is over.

Equipment and Clothing

Stick and Puck. When choosing a stick, check the length. Be sure it is the right size for you. With your skates on, stand the stick upright in front of you. The top end should come up to your chin.

You will also need a hard rubber puck. Plastic pucks, which are less expensive, are useful for practice.

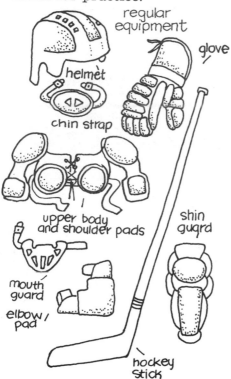

regular equipment

helmet
chin strap
glove
upper body and shoulder pads
shin guard
mouth guard
elbow pad
hockey stick

Skates. When you begin, it's worth investing in a good quality pair of hockey skates.

hockey puck
hockey skate

Be sure they fit right. Ill-fitting skates keep you from stopping and starting properly and may cause injury. They should fit tight. Your skate size will probably be the same as your regular shoe size. As your foot grows, you can trade in your skates for a larger pair at a substantial savings. Another money saver—buy second-hand ones from a reliable source. Whether they are used or not, be sure the quality and fit are good. For extra tightness, wind your laces twice around the top of the skate. A skate key is helpful in tightening the laces.

Clothing. Ice hockey requires a lot of equipment for body protection. If you play on a regular organized team, you will need the complete outfit.

If you are just playing with friends, you will need the following basic items: a helmet with face mask, hockey skates, elbow pads, and knee pads.

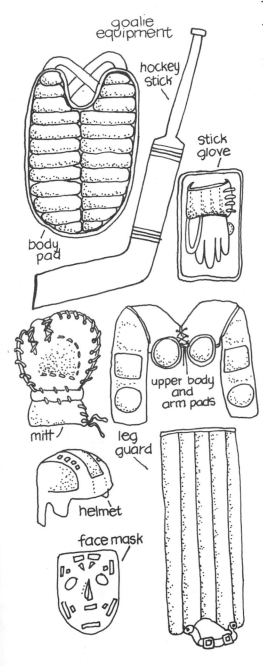

goalie equipment

hockey stick

stick glove

body pad

mitt

upper body and arm pads

leg guard

helmet

face mask

What Makes a Good Player

The most important skill in ice hockey is the ability to skate well. This means being able to skate backward as well as forward, to make sharp left and right turns, and to start and stop quickly. The balance and control of good skating demand complete body effort. Another important skill is controlling the puck with the stick.

Along with skating and stick handling, a good player must be alert, quick thinking, and able to use her common sense.

Helpful Hints

Since new equipment is very expensive, if you want to consider buying second-hand items, you can consult the bulletin board of your local rink (people who want to sell used equipment often advertise there), check your local newspaper or buying guides for the sale of second-hand equipment, or try your luck at neighborhood garage and tag sales.

It is important to take good care of your skates. Be sure to have them sharpened from time to time. Wipe off the blades thoroughly after each use. Wrap them in a cloth to protect them. Do not walk on any surface other than ice without skate guards, otherwise you will dull the blades.

Tape the blade of your stick with a moisture-resistant tape. This keeps it from getting wet or broken and is generally good protection.

Protect your helmet by wrapping and storing it in an old pillow case at the end of the season, and keep all your equipment together in one lightweight carrying bag. You will be less likely to lose things.

Good exercise for hockey are sit-ups, push-ups, and deep knee bends.

You can practice in the summer months by playing street hockey.

Where to Write for More Information

Amateur Hockey Association of the U.S.
10 Lake Circle
Colorado Springs, Colorado 80906

American Hockey Association of the United States (AHAUS) (Girls Registrars)

Massachusetts & New England
Carl Gray, AHAUS
Girls Registrar
43 Riverdale Road
Concord, Massachusetts 91742

New York
Bill Szabo, AHAUS
Girls Registrar
4950 Pine Ledge
Clarence, New York 14031

Mid-Atlantic
Kathy Bagnall, AHAUS
Girls Registrar
170 Jefferson Avenue
Cresskill, New Jersey 07626

Michigan
Barbara Lang, AHAUS
Girls Registrar
10199 Lake Side
Milford, Michigan 48042

Minnesota
Dr. Robert May, AHAUS
Girls Registrar
301 Margaret Circle
Wayzata, Minnesota 55391

Southern
John Crerar, AHAUS Registrar
P. O. Box 4208
Washington, D.C. 20012

Mid-America
Paul A. Humphrey,
AHAUS Registrar
5138 Marybrook Drive
Toledo, Ohio 43615

Rocky Mountain
Joe Rogers, AHAUS Registrar
1441 California Street
Salt Lake City, Utah 84104

Pacific
Johnny Johnson,
AHAUS Registrar
325 E. Florence Avenue
Inglewood, California 90301

Field Hockey

Field hockey gives a girl physical and mental strength . . . it can lead to a splendid, healthful life of vigor and endurance.
Constance Applebee. The "mother" of field hockey in the United States, she introduced the sport to the States.

First played in England in the mid 1800s, field hockey was introduced to America in 1901 by Constance Applebee, an Englishwoman. Fondly known as the "mother" of field hockey in the United States, she organized and taught the game for over sixty years. Applebee believed that field hockey develops willpower, determination, and endurance in

young girls, and she remained a living example of her own beliefs, coaching until she was ninety-three years old.

In other parts of the world, field hockey is played by men and women, but in the United States where it was Eleanor Roosevelt's favorite sport, it is played mostly by women. While field hockey has been an Olympic sport for men since 1932, the women's game was included for the first time in the 1980 Olympics.

One of the reasons for the popularity of field hockey is that it is an international game and therefore offers opportunities for travel and for playing teams from other countries.

Where You Play

The playing area is usually a large, smooth grassy field. It is also played on Astroturf or blacktop surfaces.

Who the Players Are

A field hockey team is made up of eleven players. The traditional lineup of the positions is

Forwards 5. Left wing, Left

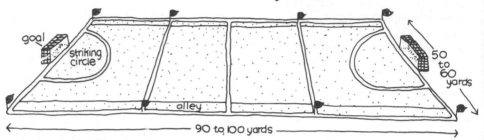

Regulation Hockey Field

goal
striking circle
alley
50 to 60 yards
90 to 100 yards

inner, Center, Right wing, Right inner. These players have the better stickwork in order to outplay the defensive players. Their job is to get the ball in a good position to score.

Halfbacks 3. Left, Center, Right. They support the forwards on offense and the fullbacks on defense. They have good timing and anticipation, which they need for intercepting and tackling the ball.

Fullbacks 2. Left, Right. They help the goalie defend the goal. They are powerful hitters who make long drives to get the ball back to their offensive players.

Goalkeeper 1. She defends the goal.

In an alternate system a coach may use her players in a variety of combinations. One example of a lineup of players is.

Forwards 4. Left outside, Right outside, Left inside, Right inside. These are the offensive players who attempt to score.

Links 2. They primarily play defense but also play offense.

Backs 3. They play defense.

Sweeper 1. The player who moves horizontally across the field in front of the defending goal. She is the team's last defense before the goalkeeper.

Goalkeeper 1. She defends the goal.

Game Talk

Bully. This action begins the game and restarts play after each goal. Two opposing players stand facing each other over a ball. After a ceremony involving the tapping of the sticks three times, the play begins as each player tries to seize the ball or pass it to a teammate.

Dodge. This means to outmaneuver an opponent while keeping control of the ball.

Dribble. Moving the ball with the stick in a series of short taps.

Drive. A sharp swinging smash of the ball.

Flick. A shot made by twisting the stick to make the ball rise and spin.

Long Corner. When the ball goes out of bounds off the endline it is brought into play from the sidelines.

Reverse Sticks. When a player changes her grip on the stick to hit the ball in a reversed direction.

Short Corner Penalty. This is when the defense fouls against the offense while in the strike circle.

Sticks. A foul made by a player who raises her stick above her shoulders to hit the

Both players fix eyes on an oncoming ball.

ball.

Tackle. By using her stick, a player takes the ball away from her opponent.

How the Game Is Played

Field hockey is played by two teams. The players move the ball along the ground by using the flat side of the field hockey stick. The object of the game is to drive the ball into the opponent's goal in order to score. Each goal is worth one point. The game is divided into two halves. There are no time-outs. Body contact is not permitted. This means no shoving, hitting, or tripping. Players may use their sticks to move the ball and tackle. They may not use them to strike or hold down an opponent's stick. The sticks cannot be raised above shoulder level at any time. Only the goalkeeper is allowed to kick the ball.

Equipment and Clothing

Ball and Stick. A regulation ball is a small hard ball, 3 inches in diameter and covered with white leather. You may also use a white composition ball, which is less expensive and good for practice.

A field hockey stick is made of wood with a blade that is flat on the left side and rounded on the right side. (There is no special blade for a left-handed player.) The stick may be 34 to 36 inches long. The way to choose the correct size is to rest the stick against the side of your leg, put your hand on your waist with your fingers pointing downward. The stick should meet the tip of your middle finger. Sticks weigh from 18 to 20 ounces. The offensive players usually use lighter sticks than the defensive players.

Clothing. The proper footwear is leather shoes with molded cleats and a pair of knee socks.

A regulation field hockey uniform is a kilt (a short skirt) and a blouse. For protection, players wear shin guards, and

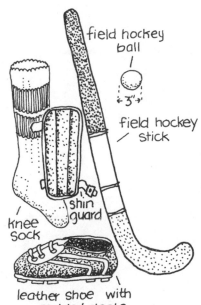

field hockey ball

field hockey stick

shin guard

knee sock

leather shoe with molded cleats

goalie

around the field at great speed. Footwork is crucial. The players take small quick steps in getting around the ball and advancing it. Strong wrists for stickwork and strong legs for speedy running are also important qualifications.

Helpful Hints

Keep your stick from drying out by rubbing it with a wood oil or Vaseline (petroleum jelly).

You can get a better grip on your stick by putting a rubber or terry cloth handle on it. These can be purchased at sporting goods stores.

When learning how to dribble, practice on the smoothest surface available. Sidewalks and blacktop surfaces are two suggestions.

A good way to practice stickwork is to play one-on-one with a friend.

Stretch your arms and legs and jog around the field to loosen up before a game.

the goalie wears leg pads and a face mask.

As a beginner you may practice and play informally in any comfortable clothing and a pair of all-court sneakers.

What Makes a Good Player

Field hockey players must be well coordinated. They have to be able to keep their eyes on the ball and know where they are going as they move the ball

Where to Write for More Information

United States Field
Hockey Association
4415 Buffalo Road
North Chili, New York 14514

Football

Although football is a rough sport, there is nothing to fear because you play against girls your own size. Football is a wonderful challenge and you get a sense of unity when playing on a team. **Linda Jefferson.** Professional football player for the Toledo Troopers.

American football had a strange and unusual beginning. It all started in England during a game of soccer at a school named Rugby. One of the players, William Webb Ellis, was frustrated when he missed a kick. He picked up the ball and ran down the field with it. His teammates were shocked and embarrassed because in

soccer players may use only their feet to move the ball. Ellis seems to have had the last laugh, because sixteen years later at the same school the game of Rugby was invented. Rugby is a combination of kicking and carrying a ball. The game was brought to America in 1871 where it was called football, and changes continued to be made through the years until it took the form of the present day game.

You may have seen women on the football field only as cheerleaders, but there are girls all over America who are playing football and loving it. And this is not new. People like Billie Jean King and a former first lady, Betty Ford, enjoyed playing football as young girls.

Football can be enjoyed on a variety of levels. It can be played with organized teams, using all the regulation equipment. As a no-tackle game at the beach, on a field, or in the park, no equipment other than the football is necessary.

Regulation football is a rough and tumble sport that involves running and tackling as well as passing and catching and kicking the ball. If you are looking for a challenging and exciting game, this could be the sport for you.

Where You Play

You can play football in any open area—your backyard, the beach, parks, fields, and vacant lots.

Who the Players Are

Offensive Team

At the Line of Play. Center 1. Snaps the ball to the quarterback. **Guards** 2. May not catch the ball—usually protect quarterback. **Tackles** 2. May not catch the ball—usually protect quarterback. **Ends** 2. May catch or run with the ball.

Backfield. Quarterback 1. She calls the play and passes, hands off, or runs with ball. **Fullback** 1. May catch or run with the ball. **Halfback** 2. May catch or run with the ball.

Defensive Team

The defense may line up any way they choose behind the line of play.

Tackles 2, **Ends** 2, **Linebackers** 2 or 3, **Cornerbacks** 2, **Safeties** 2, **Middle Guard** (if only 2 linebackers). Their job is to prevent the other team from scoring.

Game Talk

Dead Ball. This means the ball is temporarily out of play. Any movement of a dead ball does not count.

Down. An offensive play that begins at the snap of the ball and ends when the whistle stops the play.

Field Goal. Three points scored when a ball is kicked over the crossbar of the goalpost (differs from a kick made after the touchdown).

Flag Football. A variation of football in which the players snatch a flag from the ball car-

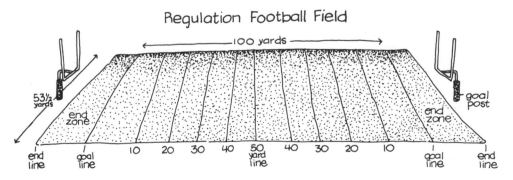

Regulation Football Field

The Toledo Troopers Women's Professional Football Team.

rier's pocket instead of tackling her.

Fumble. A ball that is accidently dropped when a player handles or runs with it. At this time, either team may try to recover it.

Huddle. When the team groups together (with the ball behind the line of scrimmage) to decide the next play.

Interception. A pass meant for a player on the offensive team but caught by a player on the defensive team.

Kickoff. When the ball is kicked by the defense of one team to the offense of the other team. The kickoff occurs at the beginning of each game, of the second half, and after points are scored.

Line of Scrimmage. The line on which the ball is placed before each play begins.

Pigskin. Another word for a football. The first footballs were made from the hides of pigs.

Punt. When the ball is dropped from the hands and kicked before it reaches the ground. In this way it is different from kicking a ball that is in a stationary position on the ground, as in a kickoff.

Safety. This is a score counting for two points, when a player is tackled behind her own goal line.

Touchdown. Six points scored by passing or carrying the ball over the opponent's goal line.

Touch Football. A variation of football in which the players merely touch the ball carrier (usually with two hands), instead of tackling her.

How the Game Is Played

Football is played by two teams. The object of the game is to score the most points by getting the football across the opponent's goal line. Points are usually earned by a touchdown, which can be scored in two ways: 1) running across the goal line with the ball and 2) passing the ball to a player on your own team on the other side of the goal. They can also be scored by safeties and field goals.

Each team is allowed four chances (downs) to move the ball at least ten yards. If they gain ten yards, they may continue to advance the ball. If they do not gain ten yards, they must turn the ball over to the other team.

Play is not continuous. It stops whenever a ball carrier is tackled, a pass is incomplete, or one of the teams scores.

The game is divided into four quarters. At the start of each quarter the team changes goals.

Although the game is called football, kicking is not the primary activity. Players are allowed to tackle, shove, and block other players.

Variations of the game include touch football and flag football. These games are played in much the same way as regular football. In touch football, the ball carriers are tagged by their opponents instead of tackled.

In flag football, all of the players wear a plastic streamer on their back pockets or belts. Instead of tackling the ball carrier, the streamer is pulled out of the pocket.

In both touch and flag football a fumbled ball is a dead ball.

These games make playing football fun and inexpensive, for they do not require equipment.

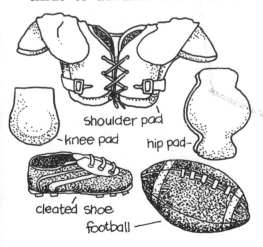

shoulder pad

knee pad

hip pad

cleated shoe

football

Equipment and Clothing

Ball. A football is an oval shaped, double-pointed ball

which is 11 inches long and weighs a little less than a pound. Its unusual shape causes it to take strange bounces, which adds to the fun of the game. The best football is made of leather, but there are good balls made of grained rubber or vinyl.

Clothing. The proper footwear for football is shoes with cleats.

In regulation play, team uniforms are worn over special body-protective equipment.

What Makes a Good Player

Football players should be strong and courageous. They must also be in good condition because the game requires a lot of stamina. You don't have to be big to play football. There are so many different skills involved that a person of any size can find a position suited to her.

Helpful Hints

Since football is a rough and tumble sport, you might want to talk the matter over with your parents before you try out for a team.

Never play hard tackle football without protective equipment. Even if it's just a neighborhood game, you should wear a helmet with a face guard, a teeth protector (mouthpiece), and shoulder and knee pads.

To throw a football properly, hold the ball close to the pointed end, with your fingers over the laces of the ball. If the ball is wet use more of the palm of your hand for a better grip.

Footwork is important to every football player. A good way to practice moving quickly is to run backward and forward at different speeds. Playing a game of tag with a friend can improve your ability to pivot and run in a zigzag movement.

Playing a fast-moving sport like basketball, which demands good wind and sharp reflexes, helps to keep you in shape for football.

Jumping rope and running in place are good indoor exercises for football.

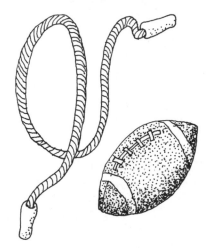

Where to Write for More Information

You may have a youth football league in your area which you can contact.

You may also write to the following addresses:

Pop Warner Junior
League Football
1315 Walnut Street, Suite 606
Philadelphia, Pennsylvania
19107

National Women's
Football League
2534 Westbrook Drive
Toledo, Ohio 43613

Punt, kick and pass contests are held throughout the United States. Information on how and where to participate is either listed in local newspapers or you can write to:

Ford Motor Company
1700 Executive Plaza
Dearborn, Michigan 48126

Lacrosse

Lacrosse is a fast moving aerial game of skill and artistry. The creativity, freedom of movement, outwitting of an opponent, and execution at the right time make Lacrosse a thrilling game and a joy to play.

Angela Tammaro. Lacrosse coach and First Vice-President of the United States Lacrosse Association.

Lacrosse is the oldest sport in North America. The Indians invented and played this rough and strenuous game as a training exercise for war. Their name for it was **baggataway.** The French Canadians were the first to learn the game from the Indians. They thought the stick the Indians used looked like a bishop's crozier. The

French word for crozier is **crosse.** So they change the name of the game to lacrosse.

This was a sport for men until the early 1900s when a separate set of rules was developed for women. Roughness and body contact were completely eliminated. The first game played by women in the United States was in 1926 at a women's college in Baltimore. Since then women's lacrosse has grown steadily in popularity in the United States and throughout the world.

Where You Play

The playing area is usually a level grassy field with two goal cages placed at either end approximately one hundred yards apart. What is unusual about this game is that there are no permanent boundaries on a women's lacrosse field. At the beginning of each game, the boundaries are decided on by the captains or coaches of the teams and the umpires. Natural markings like trees and hills are usually used. Three large circles are drawn on the field; one in the center for the draw and the other two around the goal cages.

Who the Players Are

There are twelve players on a team. The players of each team line up along the length of the field where they play one-on-one against their counterparts on the opposing team. The positions are

First Home, Second Home, Third Home, Left Attack Wing, Right Attack Wing. The main job of these players is to free themselves from their opponents in order to score. They are the best cutters on the team. The First Home is the shooting specialist who plays near the goal cage. The Second Home also plays near the goal where she tries to set the ball up in a good position to score.

Center. Although she plays both offense and defense, she is mainly a defensive player. She has to be in top physical condition to cover a large area of the field.

Third Man, Cover Point, Point, Right Defense Wing, Left Defense Wing. These players make up the defense of the team. They guard their opposing players carefully to keep them from scoring. These players are the best stick checkers on the team.

Goalkeeper. She defends the goal where she tries to prevent the other team from scoring.

Game Talk

Cutting. The skill of running in one direction, then suddenly stopping and pushing off into another direction.

Cradling. To keep the ball in the pocket of the crosse by rocking it back and forth.

Draw. This begins the game and restarts play after goals are scored. Two opposing players face each other with their crosses held at hip level and back to back. The referee places the ball between the crosses. Both players try to gain control of the ball by lift-

Regulation Lacrosse Field

ing their sticks up and away from each other.

Pull Dodge. A maneuver in which a player runs directly toward an opposing player then suddenly pulls her crosse and dodges to the left or right.

Stand. When the referee stops the play for a foul or a ball that is out of bounds, the players must stand and hold their position.

Stick-check. An attempt by one player, using her stick (crosse), to get the ball out of the opponent's crosse.

Throw-in. This is one method of putting the ball back into play: two players from opposing teams stand equal distance apart, the referee throws the ball between them, and both players try to get possession of it.

How the Game Is Played

Lacrosse is played by two teams. The object of the game is to shoot the ball past the goalkeeper and into the goal to score. All scoring shots are made from outside the circle that surrounds the goal cage. Each goal counts as one point. The players move the ball around the field by carrying it in their crosses while running, and by passing it to teammates.

The game is divided into two periods. The play is nonstop except for goals, fouls, and timeouts. When the ball goes out of bounds during a game, play is stopped and each player remains where she is. Play begins again when the referee blows the whistle.

Women's lacrosse is a noncontact sport. Players may not hold or block their opponents. They use their sticks to try to dislodge the ball from their opponent's sticks.

Equipment and Clothing

Crosse (stick). This is a long wooden stick with a pocket made of leather strips. Metal is not allowed on the crosse used in the women's game. The sticks come in varying lengths and weights. This is how you

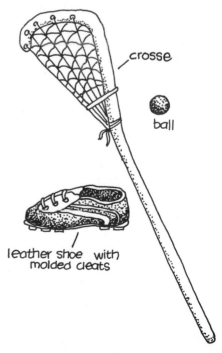

crosse

ball

leather shoe with molded cleats

54

Waiting for the action to begin.

select the right size: Put your hand on the neck of the stick, and extend your arm, holding the stick under your arm. The end of the stick should fit into your armpit and be no longer or shorter than your arm's length. The weight of the stick should be balanced: To check this, hold the stick lightly at the throat in a horizontal position. If it is balanced, it won't tip over.

Ball. A lacrosse ball is made of sponge rubber. It is 8 inches in circumference, weighs 1 1/2 to 5 ounces, and comes in a variety of colors.

Goal Cage. Goal cages for lacrosse, which are smaller than those used in soccer and field hockey, are usually supplied by the team.

Clothing. The regulation uniform is a kilt and a blouse. For practice or informal play you can wear shorts and a comfortable top. The goal-keeper wears chest and leg pads along with a face mask and helmet.

Leather shoes with molded cleats are the standard footwear.

goalie

What Makes a Good Player

A good lacrosse player prides herself on her agility and creativity on the field. The movements of this sport are flowing and graceful. Players leap to catch balls, twist to move away from opponents, and throw and catch while on the run. Every player must know how to use the crosse to scoop up, pass, catch, and cradle the ball.

Helpful Hints

Keep the leather net of your crosse in good condition by oiling it. Check frequently for small tears in the leather so you are sure your stick is in top condition for games.

When you start to use the

crosse, learn one skill at a time. The important skills are catching, throwing, and cradling.

Some of the ways you can practice using the crosse are (1) roll the ball, chase after it, and scoop it up; (2) throw the ball in the air and catch it with the crosse; (3) try to keep the ball in the pocket of the crosse while running at varying speeds.

Long distance running and sprinting are excellent ways to keep in top shape for this sport.

Where to Write for More Information

U.S. Women's
Lacrosse Association
Executive Office
P.O. Box 48
Blue Bell, Pennsylvania 19422

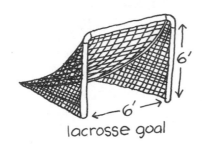

lacrosse goal

Soccer

When I play soccer I feel free. Whether I have sun, rain, or sweat on my face, I know that until the game ends, I only care about playing a good game with my teammates. I can tell you that soccer will improve your physical fitness, stamina, agility, and thinking. But most important, it's fun.
Cathie Currie. President of New York City Women's Soccer League.

One of the earliest versions of soccer was a game called harpaston played by the ancient Greeks. It was a basic kicking game in which balls filled with sand were booted around an open field. The English, however, claim that modern-day soccer began in their country. There are different stories about how and when. According to one legend, the soldiers of William the Conqueror started the game while on a drunken spree in the year 1070, when they raided a cemetery of their enemies, dug up the skulls, and began kicking them back and forth.

Today soccer is the most popular sport of all. It is played in almost every country in the world. It is called football throughout the world except in North America where it is known as soccer, probably to keep it from being confused with the American game of football. It is a Johnny-come-lately sport in the United States where girls are taking to it as readily as boys. Soccer is a thrilling sport that is easy to learn and fun to play.

Where You Play

You can play soccer on any large open field. A football field is often used.

Who the Players Are

A soccer team has eleven players. Every position is

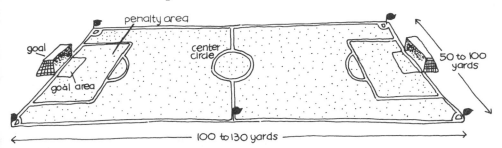

Regulation Soccer Field

penalty area

goal

center circle

goal area

50 to 100 yards

←———— 100 to 130 yards ————→

equally important to the team.

Goalkeeper. She protects the goal and tries to keep the opponents from scoring. A goalkeeper is agile and unafraid to dive to the ground or jump in the air to keep the ball out of the goal.

Fullbacks 2. Mainly defensive players, they work with the goalkeeper to defend the goal. They try to keep the ball out of their territory by stealing it and getting it to the forwards. They are good ball handlers, confident of their skills of heading and passing the ball.

Halfbacks 3. These are the runners of the team who move about the full field, playing both offense and defense. Known as the game's "playmakers," they set up plays by passing to the players who are free and in good position to score.

Forwards 5. Their job is to score, and they work at being in the right place at the right time to do so. "Wingers" is the name given to the forwards who feed the ball to the players nearest the goal. The forward who completes the play by scoring is called the "finisher" or "striker."

Game Talk

Clearing the Ball. When the ball is driven a long distance down the field.

Dribble. To control and move the ball along the ground by lightly kicking it.

Drop Ball. When the referee holds the ball at waist level and drops it to the ground between two opposing players, and each player tries to get control of the ball. A drop ball restarts play at a point near where it had been stopped.

Header. A shot or pass made by a player who hits the ball with her head.

Kickoff. A kick of the ball from the center of the field which starts the game and restarts it at halftime and after each goal is scored.

Penalty Kick. After a foul, a player from the opposing team is allowed a free kick toward the goal—a penalty kick.

Save. The goalkeeper makes a save when she stops the ball from entering the goal.

Throw-in. When the ball goes out of bounds at the sidelines, a player from the team which did not touch the ball last throws the ball back onto the field. The player must keep both feet on the ground and throw the ball from behind and over the top of her head.

How the Game Is Played

Soccer is played by two teams. The object of the game is to get the ball past the goalkeeper and into the other team's goal. Each goal scored is worth one point. The team that scores the most goals wins. What makes soccer unusual is that unlike most ball games the hands are not used to move the ball. Except for a throw-in, no player but the goalkeeper is allowed to touch the ball with her hands or arms. All other players use any other part of their body (feet, legs, chest, thighs, head) to propel the ball. Players are not permitted to trip or hold their opponents. The only contact that is allowed is shoulder to shoulder when going for a ball. An important part of the defensive

game is to try to kick the ball away from the opponents and steal their passes.

Equipment and Clothing

Ball and Goal Nets. A soccer ball is checkered, 27 inches in circumference, larger than a volleyball but smaller than a basketball.

In organized team play, goal nets are provided. For playing or practicing with friends, inexpensive goals can be bought at sporting goods stores, or you can simply mark the goal area with athletic bags or old clothing.

soccer ball

leather shoe with molded cleats

sweat sock

shin guard

Clothing. The most important article of clothing worn by a soccer player is her shoes. Since you must control the ball with your feet, you must have properly fitting shoes that can "feel" the ball. They are usually made of leather and have

Soccer player dribbles the ball past her opponents in a practice game.

molded cleats. Heavy metal cleats which can cause injury to players are not allowed.

Shorts, a shirt, knee-high stockings, and lightweight shin guards are the player's uniform. On wet and cold days it's good to wear a jersey containing some wool. In hot summer weather, light cotton is best.

What Makes a Good Player

Soccer is a game suited for the person with an average build. But it is a great equalizer, and there are positions for people with both large and small builds. Good physical condition is most important. If you are not fit when you start, you will become so as you play. The running that is involved will build up your stamina. Speed, alertness, and agressiveness on the field are part of good playing.

Helpful Hints

Keep your feet warm by wearing two pairs of socks, the cotton against the foot and the outer sock wool.

Keep your shoes in good condition by regularly cleaning the mud and grass off the cleats. If the shoes are leather, keep them from cracking by polishing with saddle soap. Dry shoes that get wet at room temperature, not on a hot radiator.

A good way for a beginner to learn how to juggle a ball without using her arms or hands is to blow up a balloon and practice hitting it with her head, chest, thighs, and legs.

You don't kick a soccer ball with your toe. Your coach will teach you how to kick and pass the ball using the different parts of your foot. When you have learned these techniques, practice them by kicking the ball back and forth with a friend.

Practice ball control by dribbling a soccer ball on your way to everyday places— school, the store, or a friend's house. On the sidewalks, of course, not in the middle of traffic.

The good soccer player who wants to keep her legs in good shape will find this a good conditioner: Alternate walking, running at all out speed, and jogging at an easy pace.

Where to Write for More Information

U. S. Soccer Federation
350 Fifth Avenue, Room 4010
New York, New York 10001

Softball

In some ways softball is the best of two worlds: it develops a player as an individual and demands that a player be skilled in a team effort.
Joan Joyce. Professional softball pitcher for the Connecticut Falcons.

On a cold day in Chicago in 1887, a man named George Hancock and his friends wanted to play a game of baseball indoors. They took up a broomstick to use as a bat, and a rolled-up boxing glove as a ball. This is how the first softball game was played.

Softball is very similar to baseball, with the only differences being those that grew out of its beginning as an indoor game: The playing area is smaller, the bat is thinner and lighter, and the ball is larger and softer. Also, in softball the ball is always pitched underhand.

There are two kinds of softball—fast pitch and slow pitch. American women play such a high level of softball that in recent years some teams have gone on international tours. Women's softball is an up-and-coming professional sport in the United States.

Junior softball play is divided into two age groups: eight to twelve and thirteen to fifteen.

Where You Play

Softball is played on a field similar to baseball except that the distance between the bases is shorter. In games played by players aged eight to twelve, the pitcher stands thirty-five feet away from home plate. In games played by players aged thirteen to fifteen the pitcher stands forty feet away from home plate.

Who the Players Are

Fast pitch and slow pitch softball are played by two teams. In fast pitch there are nine players on a team. In slow pitch there are ten players. The extra player, called a short outfielder, plays in an area behind second base.

There is only one team in the field at a time. The team in the field is called the defense and is made up of the following players:

Pitcher. She must be able to pitch the ball underhand to the batter. A strong arm and total concentration are necessary for this important position.

Infield. First Baseman, Second Baseman, Shortstop, Third Baseman. They have to be good catchers and accurate throwers. It's their job to get the batters out at the bases.

Outfield. Right Fielder, Center Fielder, Left Fielder, Short Fielder (in slow pitch only). Speed—to get around the spacious outfield—and a good throwing arm to relay the ball back to the infield, are important for these players. They catch the hard-hit fly balls and long grounders.

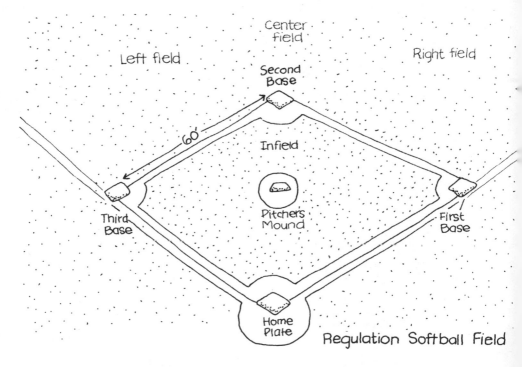

Regulation Softball Field

Catcher. She guards home plate where the runs are scored. She must also catch the pitched balls and pop flies.

Game Talk

The game talk of softball is exactly the same as in baseball (see page 24).

How the Game Is Played

As stated, softball is played like baseball (see page 26). One difference is in the pitch. In both, the fast and slow pitch is always underhand. The differences in the two games are that in slow pitch, base stealing and bunting are not allowed; in fast pitch, they are. A slow pitch ball must be thrown at a moderate speed and move in an arc on the way to the batter, whereas a fast pitch ball can be thrown as hard as the pitcher can throw.

Equipment and Clothing

Softball. It is larger than a baseball but only a little softer in spite of its name. In junior play a ball that is 12 inches in circumference and weighs 12 ounces is used. The ball is usually covered with leather, but there are softballs covered with rubber to make them waterproof.

Bat. Softball bats are thin-ner and lighter than baseball bats. A softball bat can be made of either wood or metal. Choose the one you prefer. The bats come in different lengths and sizes. Younger players may use bats from 26 to 34 inches long. The best way to select a bat for weight is to get the heaviest one that you can swing easily.

Glove. A softball glove is made of leather and has separate compartments for each finger. Some girls use baseball gloves to play. This is fine so long as the pocket of the glove is large enough to hold a softball.

Mitt. A mitt is worn by the catcher and first baseman. It is like a glove except that it has a separate compartment for the thumb only.

Clothing. Players on regulation softball teams usually wear colorful uniforms of shorts and tops. They also wear leather shoes with molded cleats. The catcher wears a face mask and a chest protector in addition to her uniform. If you don't have a uniform, you can play comfortably in jeans or shorts, a T-shirt and all-court sneakers. Team members should wear clothing of the same color to distinguish them from the team they play against. A baseball-type hat is very helpful for keeping the sun and hair out of your eyes.

What Makes a Good Player

The most basic skills for softball are strong, accurate throwing and good catching. Consistent hitting is also important. Softball is considered more of a "hitting game" than baseball, partly because the ball is larger and the bat thinner. Since running, whether to a base or after a ball, is part of the game, speed is a factor. The best softball players show quick reflexes and good concentration for this lively game.

Helpful Hints

Softballs are available in bright orange for playing at dusk.

Keep a wooden bat away from direct heat which can damage it.

The pitcher winds up for the throw.

Taping the bat handle with adhesive tape will give you a firmer grip. The tape must extend 10 to 15 inches down from the knob end of the bat.

The biggest problem beginning softball players have is throwing the ball correctly. Avoid picking up bad habits that will later have to be unlearned by asking a coach or experienced player to teach you the right way.

When alone practice catching the ball with a glove by throwing it high into the air and catching it. Close both hands around the ball as you catch it. Practice with a friend by throwing the ball back and forth on the ground and in the air. Call out "grounder" or "fly" before the throw.

Hitting and throwing plastic balls at a target can help improve your accuracy.

Always loosen up before a game by running and stretching.

A good way to relax before stepping up to bat is to take a few practice swings and loosen up your arms and shoulders.

Where to Write for More Information

To learn about rules and tournaments.

American Softball Association
2801 N.E. 50th Street
P.O. Box 11437
Oklahoma City, Oklahoma 73111

Little League Softball
Little League Headquarters
P.O. Box 1127
Williamsport, Pennsylvania 17701

Cinderella Softball League
Corner Spruce and Baker St.
Corning, New York 14830

If you are interested in learning about women's professional softball, write to a team in your area.

San Jose Sunbirds
231 O'Connor Drive
San Jose, California 95128

Bakersfield Aggies
Attention: Bob Miller
2421 Haley St.
Bakersfield, California 93305

Santa Ana Lionettes
1360 S. Anaheim Blvd.
Anaheim, California 92815

St. Louis Hummers
899 Meramec Station Road
Fenton, Missouri 63025

Buffalo Breskis
1643 Orchard Park Road
West Seneca, New York 14224

Connecticut Falcons
39 Butler St.
Meriden, Connecticut 06450

Volleyball

In volleyball you must always be ready for the unexpected. As a player you must combine intelligence to outsmart an opponent, power to spike, and quickness to set up the ball. Playing volleyball has helped me to grow up and become a more sociable person because I am always meeting new people and new challenges. **Juliete Miller.** Member of Rutgers University Volleyball Team.

Volleyball was invented in Holyoke, Massachusetts in 1895 by William Morgan, a YMCA instructor. He made up this indoor game so that older men who found other games too strenuous could have a game to play. Volleyball was devised for recreation and relaxation and combines the features of tennis and handball.

Although it was originally invented for men, women and girls began playing it in schools and recreation centers almost at once. Even so, volleyball as the first team sport for women included in the Olympics took place only in 1964.

Where You Play

A regulation court is sixty feet long, thirty feet wide, and divided in half by a net. One reason for the popularity of volleyball is that it can be played indoors or outdoors all year round and in any open place such as beaches, lawns, playgrounds, and gyms.

Who the Players Are

There are six players on each team but no set position for any of the players. Everyone plays each position. The players line up in two rows behind the net. Each row has three players. The player in the

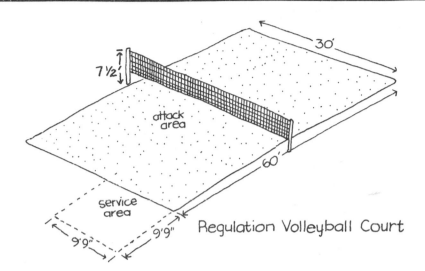

7 ½'

30'

attack
area

60'

service
area

9'9"   9'9"

Regulation Volleyball Court

right back position serves. The players rotate in a clockwise motion, so that everyone plays each position during the course of the game.

Informal volleyball is less rigid and can be played with anywhere from three to ten players on a side.

Game Talk

Ace. When a serve is not able to be returned and a point is scored.

Bump. An underarm two-handed pass in which the ball is propelled from a point between the wrists and elbows.

Dig. To save a ball by hitting it just before it reaches the ground.

Foot Fault. Stepping into the court before hitting the ball when serving.

Rotation. The clockwise movement of the players during the game when the team receives the ball for service.

Set Up. To pass the ball to another player on the same team who is in a position to strike.

Side Out. This is when the serving team loses possession of the ball.

Spike. To hit the ball into the opponent's court with a hard downward motion.

How the Game Is Played

Volleyball is played by two teams of six players each. The ball is hit back and forth over a net until it either goes out of bounds or touches the ground. The object of the game is to succeed in hitting the ball over the net so that it cannot be returned. A team is allowed to hit the ball up to three times before the ball **must** cross over the net. The first two hits are usually used to set up the ball to a teammate who tries to spike the ball into the opponent's court. Points can be scored only by the serving team. If the serving team fails to return the ball, they lose the service, and the opposing team serves. The same player serves during a team's turn. When the team regains service, all the players rotate and a new player serves.

The team that scores fifteen points first with at least a two-point lead wins the game.

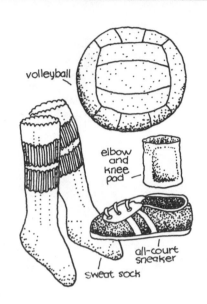

volleyball

elbow and knee pad

all-court sneaker

sweat sock

Equipment and Clothing

Volleyball. A volleyball is smaller than a basketball and a little larger than a soccer ball. A regulation ball is about 26 inches in circumference and weighs about 9 ounces.

Net. The net is 32 feet long and 3 feet wide. For regulation women's play, it is hung so that the top of the net is 7 1/2 feet from the ground. For girls aged eleven to twelve, the net is usually lowered to 6 1/2 feet above the ground. For girls aged eight to ten the net is lowered to 6 feet.

Clothing. Regulation uniforms usually include all-court sneakers, knee-high socks, shorts, a shirt, and elbow and knee pads.

Since volleyball is an informal sport, what you wear is determined by where you play. Wear what's comfortable.

What Makes a Good Player

Teamwork is very important in this game. A good volleyball player knows how to assist and set up the ball for her teammates. Each player must play all of the positions and has to be able to serve, spike, and smash the ball over the net in all circumstances. A good player is an all-around player who can move quickly and jump high. Strong arms and shoulders are a plus.

Everyone who plays volleyball should have their own ball so it can be used for practice.

Leather Ball. These are used in regulation play. They last long and are a good investment. Condition a new stiff leather ball by rubbing it with saddle soap.

Synthetic Leather Ball. If you play or practice on concrete, this is the ball to use, because a leather ball will wear out too quickly.

Rubber Ball. It's not good to practice with a rubber ball. The feel and bounce of the ball is different from a leather one. Another problem with this kind of ball is that it stings the arms.

Beginning players should learn the underhand serve first.

Jumping is one of the most important skills in volleyball play. Practice by jumping up from a squat position in sets of

Jean Champion

Volleyball players fight for a point at the net.

ten and jumping rope.

Running up long flights of stairs two at a time is a good conditioner for volleyball.

Many coaches encourage volleyball players to enter weight-training programs. If you would like to strengthen your upper body and legs in this way, be sure you do it under proper supervision.

Where to Write for More Information

American National
Volleyball Association
7201 Garden Grove Blvd.
Garden Grove, California
92641

CHAPTER 5
Individual Sports

Bicycle Road Racing

I like sports but never considered myself an athlete because I wasn't good enough to make a team. Then I discovered bicycle racing.

Mary Jane Reoch. U.S. Women's Bicycle Racing champion.

The first bicycle was made in France in the 1700s. It was a strange contraption without pedals or wheels. Over the years bicycles underwent

many changes. As they improved, the sport of cycling became more and more popular. In the 1860s, a bicycling craze took hold of America. Riding schools sprung up to teach people how to ride, and bicycle racing became the favorite Sunday pastime. Women were as active in racing as men. American women have won four world championships since 1969.

At the turn of the century, bicycling was one of the best-attended sports in America; then for a number of years it fell out of popularity. Now it is making a comeback as a competitive sport and as a leisure-time activity. There are dozens of different kinds of events from sport races to week-long competitions. Riders of all ages compete for prizes and recognition.

It's a great sport for girls because it is one of the few sports where teenagers compete equally with adults. Another plus is that the aerobic nature of the activity is perfect for controlling your weight.

Where and How to Race

Bicycle races are held in every state in the country. Almost every cycling club in the United States conducts one or more races a year. Entry blanks for races are available from clubs and bike shops, and the schedules are published in cycling magazines and local newspapers.

Road races are held on open roads and highways. The course may be over flat or hilly ground. The racers ride either from one point to another or out and back.

1800's bicycle

A favorite kind of race for beginners is the criterium, which is held on a short loop closed to traffic. The laps measure from less than a mile up to three miles. The number of laps is determined by the length of the race. Spectators enjoy criterium races because they can watch the develop-

ment of the race as the riders circle the loop.

Generally you will race with riders in your age group. The age divisions are

Midgets	Ages 8-11
Intermediates	Ages 12-14
Juniors	Ages 15-17

Game Talk

Breakaway. A rider who breaks out ahead of the main bunch.

Chasers. Riders who try to catch up to the breakaway.

Drafting. Riding close behind another racer who is fighting the air. By drafting, a rider can move at the same speed as the racer in front, but use less energy.

Kick. A final burst of speed just before the racer reaches the finish line.

Pedal Action. Easy, smooth, and strong pedaling.

Equipment and Clothing

Bicycle. You don't need an expensive racing bike to participate in road and criterium races. Any ten-speed bicycle is fine. The gears on a ten-speed bike help you to maintain speed when going uphill. Don't buy a bike that you will have to assemble yourself. Putting a bike together correctly is a difficult task. Check your local library for a bicycle buying guide

The leading cyclist in a road race.

before you make your final selection.

Helmet. A lightweight helmet is essential when racing. They are not expensive and can be bought in different sizes and colors. If your local bike shop does not carry them, the Amateur Bicycle League of America will supply you with a list of places where they can be bought.

Clothing. Shoes, gloves, and shorts are especially made for the advanced racers. But these are not required or necessary for junior racing. You can race in ordinary

76

sneakers, shorts or straight-leg tight pants, and a comfortable top. Local clubs usually give their members racing jerseys.

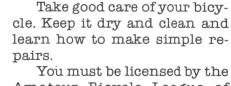
glove

What Makes a Good Racer

Bicycle racing requires strong legs, excellent wind, and good knowledge of bike control and racing tactics. Riding your bike fast for long distances is probably the best training method for beginners.

Helpful Hints

In the winter months, ice-skating is a good way to keep in shape for the bicycle racing season.

Running three times a week will improve your ability to ride up hills.

Take good care of your bicycle. Keep it dry and clean and learn how to make simple repairs.

You must be licensed by the Amateur Bicycle League of America to enter a race. Ask at your local bicycle shop for information or write to the league. The address is listed at the end of this section.

Where to Write for More Information

United States
Cycling Federation
2607 Downer Avenue
Milwaukee, Wisconsin 53211

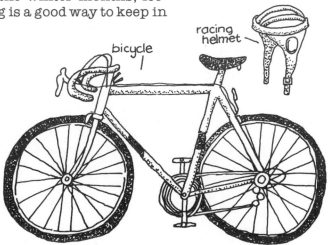
racing helmet
bicycle

Amateur Bicycle
League of America
669 Wall Street Station
New York, New York 10005

For information on bicycle tours:

America Youth Hostels
National Campus
Delaplane, Virginia 22025

An excellent source of information on cycling news and events is

Velo News
Main Street, Box 1257
Brattleboro, Vermont 05301

Bowling

Bowling is not as discriminatory as other sports. Regardless of size, big or small, you can achieve your own level of success. Your size won't limit you, only your desire. For me, bowling has been a nourishing experience both physically and mentally.

Pat Mercatanti. Pennsylvania state doubles champ and broadcast coordinator of the Women's Professional Bowling Association.

The story of bowling can be traced back to the Stone Age when cave men rolled large stones at standing targets. It was not a game then but a form of target practice for hunting. All through history people played games that were similar to bowling. A game called nine pins was brought to

America by the early Dutch settlers. It was played outdoors in an area called Bowling Green. That section of New York City still exists today. Around 1900 the game was brought indoors and a tenth pin was added. This was the beginning of modern bowling.

Bowling is a favorite sport for women. More women compete in bowling than in any other sport. Today there are many opportunities for girls to compete in tournaments on an equal basis with boys.

Where You Play

Bowling is done in regular bowling lanes which are located in almost every town in the United States. You can also practice bowling at home using inexpensive plastic bowling kits that are sold in toy stores or by setting up your own targets using old tin cans or pins and rubber balls.

Game Talk

Alley. This is the place where you bowl, also called a lane.

After throwing the ball, the young bowler keeps her eyes fixed on it as it rolls down the alley.

Frame. There are ten frames in a game. A bowler is given two chances per frame to knock down all the pins.

Foul. This is when a player steps over the foul line of the lane.

Gutter. Narrow channels on both sides of a bowling lane.

Gutter Ball. A ball which goes into a gutter before reaching the pins.

Spare. When all ten pins are knocked down with two balls in a frame.

Split. After the first roll, when pins are left standing so wide apart that a ball can roll between them without touching either one.

Strike. When all ten pins are knocked down with the first ball in a frame.

Turkey. Three strikes in a row.

How the Game Is Played

Ten pins are set up at the end of an alley, and a player rolls a ball down the alley and tries to knock down the pins. The game is divided into ten frames. Two balls are bowled in each frame unless all the pins have been knocked down in the first try. The object of the game is to score the most points by knocking down as many pins as possible. One point is scored for each pin that is knocked down. However, extra points are scored with strikes and spares. A strike is scored when all the pins are knocked down in the first roll of a frame. A strike earns ten points plus the total of pins knocked down in the next two rolls. A spare is scored when all the pins are knocked down on the second roll of the frame. The spare earns ten points plus the total of pins knocked down on the next roll. The highest score possible is 300.

The score sheet is marked in the following way:

Strike ⊠
Spare ⊘
Miss ⊟

This is a sample score sheet.

	1	2	3	4	5	6	7	8	9	10	TOTAL
Alice	8⌊1	7⌊∕	3⌊6	9⌊∕	8⌊∕	6⌊2	8⌊1	9⌊-	8⌊∕	5∕6	
	9	22	31	49	57	65	74	83	91	107	113
Margo	9⌊-	5⌊2	8⌊∕	9⌊∕	5⌊⊠	8⌊∕	5⌊2	7⌊1	9⌊∕	4⌊∕⊠	
	9	16	35	50	70	85	92	100	114	134	144
Lisa	⊠	4⌊5	7⌊2	6⌊∕	9⌊⊠	9⌊-	7⌊2	9⌊-	8⌊∕	8⌊1	
	19	28	37	56	75	84	93	102	130	139	139
Miriam	8⌊∕	⊠	9⌊-	8⌊1	⊠	⊠	8⌊∕	9⌊∕	9⌊∕	⊠7⌊2	
	20	39	48	57	85	105	124	143	163	182	191

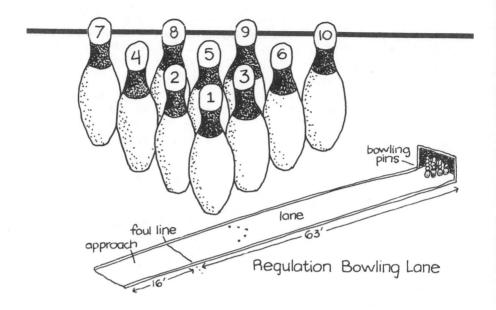

Regulation Bowling Lane

bowling pins

lane

foul line

approach

63'

16'

Equipment and Clothing

Every bowling lane supplies the equipment necessary to bowl.

Bowling Ball. The ball, 27 inches in circumference, can weigh from 6 to 16 pounds. It has two or three holes for gripping. When selecting a

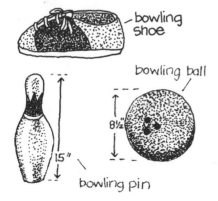

bowling shoe

bowling ball

bowling pin

8½"

15"

ball, choose the heaviest one that you can hold and throw comfortably. A beginner should start with a ball with three holes. Check the thumb fit. It should be snug enough so that the ball won't drop, but loose enough so that the thumb slips out easily. The size of the ball is correct if the knuckles of your fingers are directly over the holes.

Clothing. Players often use the shoes which are for rent at the lanes. These are standard bowling shoes. The advanced player, however, will usually buy her own regulation shoes which are sold at most bowling alleys.

There is no uniform for bowling. Wear whatever is comfortable and allows freedom of movement. If you bowl in an organized league, you will probably wear a team shirt.

What Makes a Good Player

Bowling is a simple game. Accurate aim is the single most important skill. A good bowler must develop a technique which includes: holding the ball correctly; well-timed approach steps; and a proper swing and ball release. Anyone can bowl, but a good bowler who wants to compete in tournaments must practice regularly.

Helpful Hints

In order to save your energy for the game, lift the ball from the racks with both hands.

To keep your bowling arm strong, hold the weight of the ball in the nonbowling hand until the moment you take your first step.

Select a ball from the rack that is comfortable. Look for markings or numbers on the ball that will help you identify it as yours.

Good manners when bowling are important. A rule to remember is that the person on your right has the "right of way." This means if you are both starting at the same time, he or she should be allowed to roll first.

Because of the way the balls are made, the same ball can be used by right- and left-handed people.

Ask at your local bowling lanes for information about lessons and tournaments.

Where to Write for More Information

American Junior
Bowling Congress
5301 South 76 St.
Greendale, Wisconsin 53129

Distance Running

Through your own efforts as a runner, you can have a great sense of accomplishment, and from that comes incredible self-confidence.

Kathrine Switzer. Runner who broke the sex barrier at the Boston Marathon.

Running is a natural human activity. Throughout history man has run both for survival and for the fun of it. Distance running has exploded into one of the most popular sports in America. The

marathon, one kind of distance event, originated in ancient Greece in 490 B.C., when Pheidippedes, a Greek soldier, ran all the way from Marathon to Athens to tell of the Greek victory over the Persians. After announcing the victory, he fell dead. He had run a distance of 26.2 miles. A marathon, a road race of this distance, commemorates this legendary feat.

Women have had to struggle to prove that running is as normal for them as it is for men. Years ago women were allowed to compete only in short races. It was believed that they were incapable of running long distances. Today women regularly run long distances, and it is an accepted fact that they are better built for the endurance of a long race than a short race.

Now that running has become so popular in America, races are being held all over the country and throughout the year. Girls and women are competing in these races in ever-increasing numbers.

Where and How to Race

Any race over two miles is considered a distance race. The usual distance of a road race ranges from 2 miles to 26.2 miles. A marathon is 26.2 miles, a half-marathon is 13.1 miles, and there are various races from 2 to 13 miles. One of the most popular events for young people is the 6.2 mile race also known as a 10 kilometer race. Authorities recommend that adolescents not compete in races longer than 13.1 miles.

Most races are open to all runners. Some are specialties open only to certain groups such as families, women, and youngsters.

To register officially in a race, you must sign up in advance. You will be given a number to wear, and your time will be recorded. Registering for a race is easy. You merely fill out a simple application and mail it in before the deadline date. To guarantee that a reply is sent to the right name, enclose a stamped envelope with your name and address. Most races require advanced registration. Sometimes it is possible to register a few hours before the race begins. Whatever the case, be sure you know the requirements of the race you want to run in.

Racing events are publicized in local newspapers and storefront windows. If you like to plan ahead, you can obtain a year's schedule of races from the nearest Road Runners Club.

Game Talk

Jog. A slow run.

Fartlek. A method of training that combines moderate running with frequent short bursts of speed.

Fun Run. Races of two to six miles where no awards are given and no times recorded.

LSD (Long Slow Distance). A method of training: long runs at a slow pace.

Pace. To run in a manner that spreads your energy throughout the race.

Equipment and Clothing

Shoes. The only equipment for this sport is a good pair of running shoes. They are designed to give your feet the best support and protection when running. A running shoe is made with a thick-layered sole and an elevated heel to cushion the impact of constant foot pounding.

When buying running shoes, go to a sporting goods store or a store that specializes in athletic shoes. They offer the best selection and sales people

Runners in the all-female, 6.2 mile annual race in New York City's Central Park.

who are trained to give you a proper fit. The shoe should feel comfortable and fit snugly. It should hug your heel and mold the widest and narrowest parts of your foot. Keep in mind that your foot swells when running. Allow for a half-inch of space between your longest toe and the tip of the shoe. To test, press your thumb down on top of the shoe while your foot is inside. If your thumb lies down neatly, you have a good fit.

Important: A good thick pair of sweat socks on your feet absorbs moisture and gives added cushioning.

running shoe

athletic sock

Clothing. You can wear any clothing you want when running. However, comfort is an important consideration and you should avoid tight-fitting clothes. In cold weather sweat pants or warm-up pants are good leg coverings. Wear a long-sleeved cotton T-shirt on top with a jacket that unzips in front because you can get very warm while running even when it's cold outside. Cover your head with a snug-fitting hat or hood because body heat escapes through the head. Light cotton gloves will keep your hands warm. You might find it more handy to wear cotton socks on your hands. They work like mittens. In warm weather, nylon or cotton shorts and loose-fitting sleeveless tops are best.

What Makes a Good Runner

Even though running is the easiest and most natural of all sports, successful racing depends on the training you do before the race and how you pace yourself during the race.

Training is a simple matter of putting in the time running. Run long rather than fast. You will increase your speed naturally. A unique aspect of distance running is that anyone who has the self-confidence to enter a race and complete it is a winner. Finishing first is not as important as running the race in the best time for you.

Helpful Hints

Training

Don't run on your toes when running long distances.

Run relaxed. Your heel should hit the ground first as the rest of your foot rolls forward. Let your arms hang loose at your sides (waist level) so they can swing naturally. Don't clench your fists.

When training, run at a comfortable pace. You should be able to talk to yourself or to a running companion or whistle as you run.

When you go out for a run, carry a dime in case you need it for a phone call. Better yet, carry two dimes in case of misdialing or a faulty phone.

Let your body cool down after a run. End the run a block or two before you reach home and walk the rest of the way.

Racing

Gear up for the race by packing a bag that includes a bottle of water for drinking and washing, a towel to wipe off sweat, and petroleum jelly to ease the discomfort of skin chafing.

If possible, try to run the route of the race sometime before the big day. Being familiar with the course and knowing you can run the distance will give you added confidence.

In running a long race, the temptation is always to start out fast . . . Don't. It's better to start at a comfortable pace. You can always speed up if you start too slow. But you may not finish if you start too fast.

To make certain that you have enough fluids in your system on the day of the race, drink a pint of liquids—water is best—one half hour before the race. If you are running a long race, don't wait until you are thirsty to drink. Water is provided along the route, and you should pause for a few sips as you go along.

Where to Write for More Information

For more information and locations of local or regional running clubs, write to.

Road Runners Club of America
8605 Acorn Circle
Vienna, Virginia 22180

Golf

Golf is the greatest sport. People of all sizes can play. It takes you outdoors where it's you against the course.
Sandra Palmer. Professional golfer.

Over two thousand years ago the Romans played a game called **paganica** in which they hit a feather-stuffed ball with a bent stick. When the Romans conquered the British Isles they brought this game with them. Five hundred years later "golfie," a game very similar to paganica, was popularized by the people of Scotland. Golfie, or golf, was enjoyed by Mary Queen of Scots, the first famous woman to play the game. She originated the word caddy by calling the boy who carried the clubs and sighted the balls **cadet,** which is French for student. The word caddy is still used today to describe the person who assists golfers.

By the 1880s, golf had spread to the United States, and an American woman played for the first time in 1889. One of the reasons for the popularity of golf is that it can be played by anyone from the age of eight to eighty. Golf is truly an individual sport in which the opponent is the course instead of another player and the golfer sets her own pace and her own goals.

Where You Play

Golf is played on a course which has nine or eighteen holes. Each hole is made up of these places:

Tee. The area from which the ball is hit at the beginning of play.

Fairway. The mowed area between the tee and the green.

Green. The plot of close-cut grass at the end of each fairway that surrounds the hole.

To challenge the player, each course has obstacles such as sand traps, hills, and streams.

Good places to practice golf are driving ranges and putting greens, which are found in many areas. A small fee has to be paid to use these facilities.

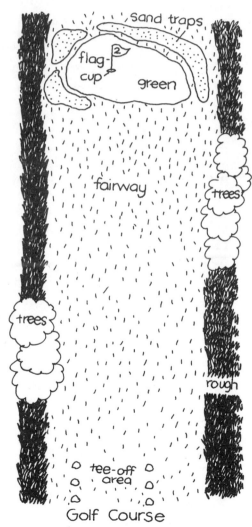

Golf Course

Birdie. To score one less than par for the hole.

Bogey. To score one more than par for the hole.

Bunker. One kind of obstacle used in the course, often a sand trap.

Divot. A slice of grass dug up from the fairway after swinging the club.

Eagle. To score two less than par for a hole.

Fore. A warning cry to players to watch out for the ball coming their way.

Handicap. A number rating given to a player. It is based on the player's best average score and the par for the course.

Hole. The target into which the ball falls.

Par. Each hole on a golf course has a rating called par. Par is the number of strokes in which an expert player would make that hole.

Rough. The high grass surrounding the fairway.

How the Game Is Played

The object of the game of golf is to hit the ball into the hole in each of the nine or eighteen holes of a course in as few strokes as possible. When playing in groups of two to four players, each player takes a

Jane Silver

A young golfer "tees up" for practice.

turn, playing with her own ball. Each swing at the ball is a stroke and is counted whether the ball is touched or not. If the ball is driven out of bounds or off the course, a penalty of an added stroke is given. When this happens, a substitute ball is played from the same spot. The player with the lowest score is the winner.

Players compete against each other. When playing alone, a golfer competes against par.

Equipment and Clothing

The basic equipment needed for golf is expensive. When you are just beginning, borrow or rent your clubs. If you have no other way to come by a set, buy second-hand clubs.

Clubs. Two basic kinds of clubs are needed for the game. They are woods and irons. The woods are used for long shots, to cover distance, and the irons are used for shorter shots that require accuracy. Each club has a number. A beginner's set of clubs would include

2 woods: numbers 1 and 3,
5 irons: numbers 3, 5, 7 and 9,
and one putter.

Ball. A golf ball is a small, hard, white dimpled ball. You will need at least three golf balls when you first play. Because they are expensive and beginners lose them easily, it's

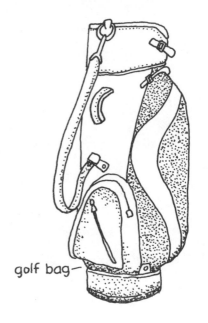

golf bag

a good idea to buy used ones. Plastic balls are commonly used for backyard practice. They are available at sporting goods stores.

Tees. These are small wooden or plastic pegs on which the ball is placed to start the play. They are inexpensive and you will only need two or three of them.

Bag. You need a bag to carry your clubs. It should be lightweight and have a pocket to hold the balls and tees.

Clothing. Many players find that wearing a golf glove helps avoid blisters. A right-

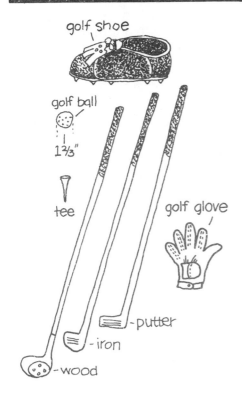

golf shoe

golf ball

1⅔"

tee

golf glove

putter

iron

wood

the ball in such a way that it rolls along the green and into the hole. Technique, accuracy, and strength are qualities of a good golfer. Golf is like two games in one. A golfer should also be a good walker, since about two miles have to be covered when playing a round of nine holes.

Helpful Hints

Good manners are an important part of golf.

● You should ask faster or more experienced players to play through first.

● The player whose ball is farthest from the cup putts first.

● Dragging your bag on the greens will destroy the turf.

● Never talk to someone who is hitting the ball.

● If you dig up clumps of grass (divots) when swinging, be sure to replace them.

● If your ball goes in the direction of other golfers, warn them by calling FORE.

To keep from losing clubs, count them after playing each hole.

When you play in the rain or on wet grass, dry your clubs before putting them back in your bag.

You can make your game more fun by playing on a team or entering tournaments.

If you want to practice in

handed golfer wears the glove on the left hand. When you are past the beginner stage, you might want to invest in a pair of golf shoes. The spikes on the soles prevent slipping. Wear clothes that are comfortable and suitable for the weather.

What Makes a Good Player

The first skill a player must have is the ability to swing a club that will hit the golf ball long distances. Secondly, a player must be able to putt well, which means to stroke your own backyard, try this easy way of making a putting green. Cut the grass very low in a small area of the yard. Dig a hole in the middle of the area and sink an empty tin can into it.

Where to Write for More Information

Ladies Professional
Golf Association
919 Third Avenue
New York, New York 10020

United States Golf Association
Golf House
Far Hills, New Jersey 07931

Racket Sports
Tennis

I chose to play tennis because I like to run and hit a ball. Also, there is a great deal of spontaneity in the game because the ball never comes over the net twice in the same way.
Billie Jean King. Professional tennis player.

Tennis, the best known racket sport, was invented in England in 1873 by Walter Wingfield. He took some of the features of court tennis, a game which was played indoors, and brought it outdoors where it was played on a grass lawn. It

was called tennis-on-the-lawn at first, and later became known as lawn tennis. Today it is simply called tennis.

In 1874, a year after the game was invented, an American woman, Mary Outerbridge saw the game played by the British in Bermuda and liked it. She learned the rules, bought the equipment, and returned to New York where she introduced the game to the United States.

Tennis was a sport women were serious about from the beginning. In 1959, Helen Wills was the first woman to be voted into the Tennis Hall of Fame. In more recent times Billie Jean King has been responsible for bringing a higher level of respect and pay to the women's game.

Where You Play

Tennis is played on indoor and outdoor courts. The surface of the court can be either asphalt, concrete, shale, clay, or composition. Grass used to be the most popular surface,

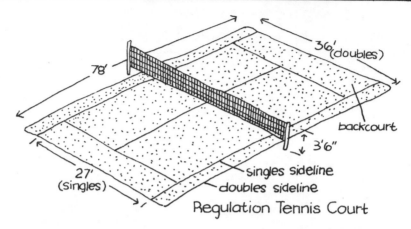

78'

36' (doubles)

backcourt

3'6"

singles sideline

doubles sideline

27'
(singles)

Regulation Tennis Court

but it is rarely used today.

Game Talk

Ace. A serve which the receiver is unable to return.

Ad-in. A term used in scoring that means advantage to the server after deuce.

Ad-out. A term used in scoring that means advantage to the receiver after deuce.

Backhand. The stroke used to hit a ball that comes to a right-handed player on her left side and vice versa.

Double Fault. Two serves that don't go into the service court. When this happens the receiver gets a point.

Drop Shot. A softly hit shot that barely travels over the net.

Fault. A serve that does not land in the service court.

Foot Fault. In service, a fault caused by the server by stepping on or over the base-line before hitting the ball.

Forehand. The stroke made on the right hand side of the body by right-handers, on the left hand side of the body by left-handers.

Half-volley. A shot in which the ball is hit just after it bounces in the court.

Let. A service point that has to be replayed because the ball touches the net before it lands in the service court.

Lob. A high arching shot that is hit into the opponent's back court.

Rally. To hit the ball back and forth during the playing of a point after the ball has been served.

Volley. A shot in which the ball is hit before it bounces into the court.

Serve. (Service) The stroke that puts the ball into play at the beginning of each point.

Smash. A hard overhead

Jane Silver

Making a forehand shot.

shot in which the racket is brought down fast on a high ball.

How the Game Is Played

Singles is played by two players using rackets to hit the ball across the net. The object of the game is to hit the ball into the opponent's court in such a way that it cannot be returned. The ball is put into play with the **service:** one player stands behind her own baseline and hits the ball over the net into her opponent's service court—the area in which she receives the ball. She has two chances to make a successful serve. Serves are alternated on each point, first into the right and then into the left service court. Players serve for a game one at a time with

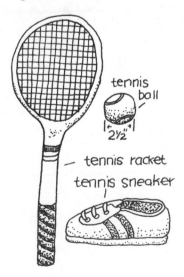

tennis
ball

2½"

tennis racket

tennis sneaker

the serve going to the other player in the next game. Once the ball is in play, the players hit it back and forth over the net until one of the players is unable to return it. Both the receiving and serving sides can score points. A player earns points when her opponent fails to return the ball properly.

Scoring is unique in tennis because it combines words and numbers. Scoring is as follows:

Zero is called love.
The 1st point you win is 15.
The 2nd point you win is 30.
The 3rd point you win is 40.
The 4th point you win ends the game.

When the game is tied at 40, it is called deuce. The next point won is called advantage. If the player with advantage wins the next point, she wins the game; if the opposing player wins the next point, the score goes back to deuce.

The first player to win six games with a two-game lead wins a set. The first player to win two sets wins the match.

Doubles is played by four players, two partners on each side. The full court, which includes the two side alleys, is used for play.

Equipment and Clothing

Racket. The most popular racket frames are made of metal or wood and are strung with either nylon or cat gut. They come in different weights and grip sizes. The weights are usually designated light, medium or heavy. The grip size is a number (like 4 1/2) that indicates the inches in circumference of the handle. Both of these markings are found on the handle of the racket. When beginning, choose a racket that is relatively light and easy to hold. Using a large heavy-handed racket will prevent you from swinging properly. To test for the proper grip size, hold the racket in a manner that is like shaking hands with it. If your thumb meets the first knuckle of the second finger, you have the right grip size for you. If the thumb overlaps, the grip is too small. If the thumb does not meet the knuckle the grip is too large.

Balls. A tennis ball is a hollow rubber ball with a fuzzy cloth cover of yellow, white, or orange. Start with a can of three new balls. It's difficult to learn how to play with old, worn-out balls.

Clothing. Tennis dresses or shorts and a top are the most popular tennis wear. The traditional color is white; however tennis clothes come in a variety of colors. It's best to wear light colors that reflect the sun's heat and are cooler. Wear tennis sneakers which are made to protect the courts and prevent you from slipping. The shoes are made of canvas or leather. Leather lasts longer but canvas is lighter and cooler. A sun visor will keep the sun out of your eyes and terry cloth wrist bands prevent perspiration from running down into your palm.

What Makes a Good Player

There are three important ingredients to playing good tennis: the footwork, which involves running and jumping; the arm work, which includes knowing how to swing the racket correctly; head-work—clear thinking and constant concentration.

Helpful Hints

Good manners are important on the court. Never walk behind someone else's court when the ball is in play. Don't throw your racket on the ground when you make a bad shot.

When you are serving first, call the score, be sure your opponent is ready, and have two tennis balls at hand.

One good way to improve your stroke is to practice hitting the ball against a wall. Another way is to practice with a ball machine. They are often for rent at indoor courts.

It's a good idea to take lessons when learning this sport. Tennis is a highly skilled game, and this will put you on the right track from the beginning. The lessons don't have to be expensive. Sometimes they are given free through local recreation departments.

Keep your racket covered to protect the strings from getting wet or broken and store the racket in an upright position.

Take a terry cloth towel with you when you play in hot weather. You can hang it on the netpost so it is handy for wiping perspiration off your face, hands, and racket handle between games.

Where to Write for More Information

United States
Tennis Association
729 Alexander Road
Princeton, New Jersey 08540

(Information about starter tennis programs and tournaments)

Pamphlet on General conditioning for tennis, write to

Tone Tennis
Box 29034
Phoenix, Arizona 85038

For a women's tennis scholarship guide, write to

College Tennis Guide
729 Alexander Road
Princeton, New Jersey 08540

Platform Tennis

Platform tennis is my favorite sport. One of the most important things I've learned is how to play with my partner as a team. We help each other out if one of us is having a bad day and encourage each other on the court during a game. It's fun to be able to go away just with your partner on weekends to tournaments. But even if you're not a tournament player, it's fun to go out with a few friends and play. Its great exercise.

Megan Foster. Winner of the 1979 American Platform Tennis National Championship (for girls 15 and under).

Platform tennis was invented in Scarsdale, New York in 1928 by James Cogswell and Fessenden Blanchard, avid tennis players who wanted a game they could play outdoors in the winter months. Their solution was to build a raised wooden platform and enclose it with a chicken wire fence, and use paddles and slow-bouncing balls.

The game is a combination of several racket sports, including tennis, badminton, and squash. It is called "paddle" for short and is therefore often confused with paddle ball, which is a different sport.

Platform tennis is unknown in some parts of the United States, but with increasing interest in racket sports, it is gaining in popularity.

Where You Play

Platform tennis is played outdoors (usually in the fall or winter) on raised wooden or aluminum platforms. Recently, some indoor courts have been built on ground level with a concrete floor. There is always a screen enclosure for the court, which is only half as big as a tennis court.

Game Talk

Corner Shot. A ball hit hard enough to rebound off the opponent's back court and usually hitting both wires where the screens meet.

Foot Fault. When the server steps over the baseline before the paddle hits the ball. This is a foul and a point goes to the opponent.

Seam. The place where the side and back screens join. It is a good place for a player to aim for because the ball will have an irregular bounce when coming off the seam.

Wires. Also called screens or fencing. A ball can be played off the wires if it first bounces in the court.

How the Game Is Played

Platform tennis is played and scored the same as tennis (see page 98) except for these differences:

The server is allowed only one serve.

A ball that bounces into the court and then off the wire fence is considered to be in play and can be hit back over the net. It is this feature of playing the rebounds that makes this game special.

The game is almost always played as doubles—which means two players oppose two other players.

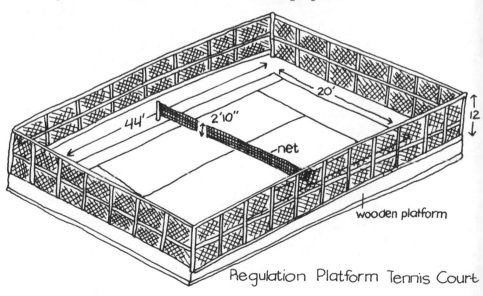

Regulation Platform Tennis Court

Equipment and Clothing

Paddle. The paddle for platform tennis, oval in shape and perforated with small holes, is made of wood or aluminum. The rim of a wooden paddle has a plastic or metal edge to protect it when it hits the wire screens. Paddles measure from 16 1/2 inches to 17 inches long and are available in a variety of weights. The lightweight "junior" models are 14 to 16 ounces. Check the bottom of the face of the paddle

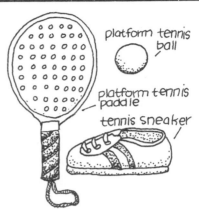

platform tennis ball

platform tennis paddle

tennis sneaker

to be sure it is stamped APTA approved. This way you can be sure you have the correct paddle for platform tennis.

APTA (1979) Junior Championship (15 and under) winners—Megan Foster and Claire Slaughter.

Ball. The balls are nearly the same size as tennis balls and are made of solid sponge rubber in bright yellow or orange.

Clothing. Since platform tennis is a winter sport usually played outdoors, the clothing should be warm but loose fitting. Long pants and several layers of tops are recommended. As the playing heats up you'll be able to shed some of the layers.

As far as footwear is concerned, tennis sneakers with natural rubber soles are best.

What Makes a Good Player

Platform tennis is one of the easiest racket sports to learn. While there is less running than in tennis, a good deal of stamina is required to play the ball off the wires. It also helps to have sharp reflexes and to be quick of foot. Strategy is the key to this game.

Where to Write for More Information

If you are interested in playing in regulation tournaments, write

The American Platform
Tennis Association
52 Upper Montclair Plaza
Upper Montclair, New Jersey
07043

The American Professional
Platform Tennis Association
527 East 72nd St.
New York, New York 10021

Table Tennis

Table Tennis can be played by anyone tall enough to see over the edge of the table. Beginners have fun just getting the ball over the net, but advanced players require reflexes, footwork, and control. I chose table tennis because it was more fascinating than all the other racket sports.

Leah "Ping" Neuberger. The greatest woman table tennis player in the history of the U.S. who now serves as the historian of the United States Table Tennis Association.

Table tennis, a highly respected international sport, is second only to soccer in worldwide popularity. The exact origin of the game is not known, but according to some records a crude form of table

tennis was played in England in 1890. Homemade materials were used and a row of books was laid across the table to make a "net."

Table tennis is also known as "Ping-Pong." It got this name from the sound of the ball in play. The ball "pings" when it bounces off the table and "pongs" when it hits the paddle.

There are many opportunities for play in leagues, clubs, and tournaments. Many countries, including the United States, conduct national championships. This is one of the few sports that awards equal prize money to men and women in the nationals.

Where You Play

The court used in this sport is a table.

A regulation table is nine feet by five feet and thirty inches high. The net stretches across the width of the table and is six feet long and six inches high. The table is dark green in color with a white line

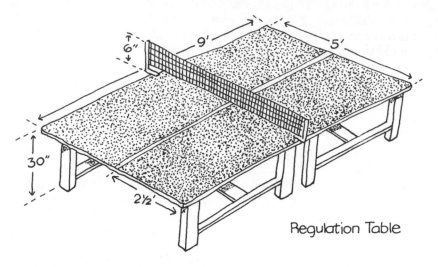

Regulation Table

which runs lengthwise down the center. This line divides the table for doubles play. It is most important that the table be firm and all the screws securely fastened. Players are not allowed to move the table during play.

Game Talk

Bat. Another name for "racket" or "paddle."

Normal Ball. A ball hit with no spin.

Pimples. The tiny bubbles on the rubber surface of the paddle.

Shake-Hands Grip. A common style of gripping the paddle that is similar to a handshake.

Topspin. A stroke that makes the ball spin toward the opposing player. The ball tends to pick up speed as it moves.

Volley. A return of the ball before it hits the table. Except in serving, no player may hit a ball before it bounces on the table.

How the Game Is Played

Singles. A game of singles is played by two players. The object of the game is to hit the ball so that it lands on the opponent's side of the table at a point where she cannot return it. Play begins with one player serving the ball so that it strikes first the server's side of the table, and then the opposite side. After the serve, the ball may strike the table only once, on the opposite side of the net. Play goes on until one player is unable to make a good return. Points are scored by both the

A young player in table tennis tournament.

server and the receiver. The players alternate service after five consecutive points are scored. The game is played until one player scores twenty-one points. If the game is tied at twenty, each player alternates service until one player wins by a two-point lead.

Doubles. Doubles is played by four players. The center white line that runs down the length of the table marks the service court by dividing it into right and left courts. Serves are made from the right-hand court of the server to the left-hand court of the receiver. The players follow a sequence in hitting the ball. The sequence is: server to receiver to server's partner to receiver's partner, and so on. After the initial serve, the ball may bounce on either side of the center line.

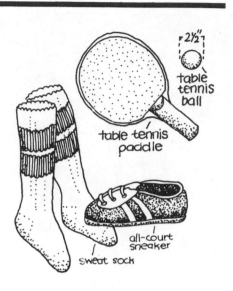

table tennis ball

table tennis paddle

all-court sneaker

sweat sock

Equipment and Clothing

Paddle. A paddle may be any size, shape, or weight. The head of the paddle is always made of wood and may be covered or uncovered. The usual covering is pimpled rubber. Buy a paddle that you can grip comfortably.

Balls. The balls are hollow and made of plastic and are about 1 1/2 inches in diameter. It's a good idea to have two or three balls at hand in case the

ball you use becomes cracked or dented.

Clothing. Dark clothes are recommended because the small white ball is difficult to see against light-colored clothes. Shorts or a skirt with a top are usually worn in competition. Socks and sneakers are the most comfortable footwear.

What Makes a Good Player

Most people think it's easy to play table tennis, but it is a demanding sport to play competitively. To be a serious player you have to be in top physical condition. You need both stamina and balance to play well. You also need to be levelheaded, because losing your temper can easily cost you a game.

Where to Write for More Information

National Junior Table
Tennis Foundation
31 Huntington Bay Road
Huntington, New York 11743

U.S. Table Tennis Association
3466 Bridgeland Drive
Saint Louis, Missouri 63044

Speed Ice-Skating

I loved racing competition because it was a test of my preparation and determination. It wasn't necessary to win to gain satisfaction from a competition. In fact, I'm sure I lost many more races than I won during my skating career. Defeat was not a failure, it was a challenge to better my performance.
Sheila Young Ochowicz. Olympic gold medalist.

The first ice skates were made of bone taken from the ribs of deer and oxen and honed into blades. Such skates were used by the Scandinavians in the year 200 as a way of getting across frozen lakes and rivers.

In the fourteenth century the bones were replaced by waxed wood, and more and more people took to skating for fun. It wasn't long before races were held. As the popularity of the sport grew, wooden blades were replaced with metal to allow for greater speed.

In 1932 women's speed skating was merely an exhibition event at the Winter Olympics, but in 1960 it became an official event.

Oddly enough one town in the United States has been the center for speed skating champions—Northbrook, Illinois, which has been called the "Speed Skating Capital of the World." It has produced such Olympic champions as Anne Henning and Diane Holum.

Where and How to Race

There are two kinds of speed races. The mass-start race, most common in the

United States, and the European-style, which is used in the Olympics. In a mass-start race, all the competitors begin together, and the first one to cross the finish line wins. In the European-style race, two skaters skate at one time in separate lanes. The skaters race against the clock instead of each other. The person with the fastest time after all the skaters have raced is the winner. Races are held both at indoor and outdoor rinks.

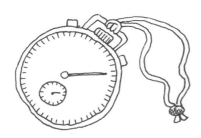

Rules govern, and a skater who pushes, trips, or interferes with another skater in any way is disqualified from the race. On the turns, the lead skater gets the inside lane.

There are separate races for girls and boys. The age groups and the distances of the races for the girls are

Pee Wee. 7-year-olds and under—100 and 200 meter races.

Pony. 8- and 9-year-olds —200 and 300 meter races.

Midget. 10- and 11-year-olds—400 and 500 meter races.

Juvenile. 12- and 13-year-olds—600 and 800 meter races.

Junior. 14- and 15-year-olds—1 mile race.

Game Talk

Bell Lap. This is the last lap of a race. A bell is rung when the lead skater crosses the line to begin the last lap.

Heat. One of a series of elimination races which are held when there are too many competitors to race at one time.

Lap. A lap is one complete turn around the rink. The number of laps you skate depends upon the length of the race.

Pack. A group of racers skating in a bunch behind the skaters who are in the lead.

Equipment and Clothing

Skates. Speed skates look something like hockey skates. The big difference is in the blade. The blades of speed skates are thin and very long (14 1/2 to 15 inches). The boots are made of lightweight leather. A new pair of speed skates costs about as much as a good pair of hockey skates. You can save money by buying used ones. You will also need a pair of skate guards to protect the blades of your skates.

leather glove

racing helmet

speed skating boot

Sharpening Kit. A sharpening kit includes a jig which holds the skates, a sharpening stone, a burr stone, and a light oil, like kerosene, for lubricating the blade. Speed skaters sharpen their blades before practice and between each race. Sharpening, which is done by hand, is not difficult. Your coach or another speed skater can show you how.

Clothing. A nylon skating suit or lightweight warm-up suit is usually worn. Some skaters prefer to wear woolen ballet-type tights which can be bought at stores that sell dance clothing. A thin, long-sleeved top is worn with the tights.

You will also need a pair of leather gloves and a lightweight protective helmet. The helmet, like the one used in bicycling, can be bought at skate and bicycle shops.

What Makes a Good Racer

To be a good racer you must first know how to skate well. Then you need to acquire the techniques of racing, which include learning how to push off at the start, to skate in a crouch position, and to swing your arms in order to increase your speed.

Helpful Hints

Your skates are an important investment. Take good care of them. Wipe the blades after each use to prevent rusting. Carry a small washcloth in your skates for this purpose. When the boots get wet, unlace them, open the tongue, and let them dry naturally.

The best ice condition for speed skating is cold, hard ice. When the air is warm the ice softens and it is necessary to skate harder to increase speed.

Avoid getting chills after the race by wrapping yourself up in something warm.

During the summer months bicycling is the best

Alice Siegel

A racer sharpens skates before a race.

way to stay in shape for speed skating. Sheila Young, who trained for speed skating by bicycling, won world titles in both speed skating and bicycle racing.

Where to Write for More Information

To find out where you can learn to speed skate, write to

Ice Skating Institute
of America
1000 Skokie Blvd.
Wilmette, Illinois 60091

For information about competitions, write to

Amateur Skating Union of the United States
4432 West Deming Place
Chicago, Ill. 60639

Speed Roller-Skating

I love the speed of roller-skate racing. It's a great sport for girls to try because it's really fun. If you join a team, you can get a chance to travel and compete, and if you practice, you can become a winner.

Caroline Row. Three-time divisional winner in the Eastern Speed League Championships.

Roller-skating racing came of age in 1979 when it was included in the Pan American Games for the first time. The sport has traveled a long and bumpy road since its birth over 350 years ago. In the seventeenth century an anonymous Dutch ice skater grew impatient waiting for the water in the canals to freeze over. He tried to substitute "ground skates" for ice skates by attaching large wooden spools to his shoes. Apparently his idea did not catch on, because nothing more was heard of roller skates until 1763 when a Belgian, Joseph Merlin, invented skates with metal wheels. His roller skates were not a success, because skaters could not turn or stop on them. They could only travel straight ahead.

It wasn't until 1863 when J.L. Plimpton, an American, devised a new skate that roller-skating became practical. It was called the "rocking skate" and could be easily guided at the skater's will. The invention of this skate touched off a worldwide boom in roller-skating and earned Plimpton the title, father of modern-day roller-skating.

Today, roller-skating is a recreational activity as well as a competitive sport. Speed skating, which is one branch of the sport, should not be confused with a Roller Derby, a rough and often violent event.

Where and How to Race

Roller-skating races are held indoors at regular roller-skating rinks. In a typical race the competitors line up three feet behind the starting line. When the official calls "to your mark" the skaters move to the starting line and take their positions. They do not move until a gunshot sounds to start the race. Anyone who pushes, holds, or trips another skater is disqualified from the race.

Girls and boys compete in separate races except for the mixed relays, which races are divided into the following categories:

Primary. Under 8 years —200, 300, and 400 meters.

Juvenile. 8 to 10 years— 200, 300, and 400 meters.

Elementary. 10 to 12 years—300, 400, and 500 meters.

Freshmen. 12 to 14 years—300, 500, and 1000 meters.

In a standard-size roller rink a 200 meter race is two laps around the rink, a 300

meter race is three laps around the rink and so forth.

If you want to compete in roller-skating races, you must be a member of the United States Amateur Confederation of Roller Skating. Begin by asking at your local rink if there is a skating club, or write to the USAC about clubs near your home. These clubs provide coaches, training, and information on racing events.

Game Talk

Block. A foul made when a racer weaves from side to side in order to prevent another skater from passing.

Corner Judge. Also known as the pylon judges. They station themselves at the pylons and watch for fouls.

False Start. Crossing the starting line before the sound of the gun that starts the race.

Free Roll. A term that describes coasting on skates.

Lap Card Holder. The official who holds up numbered cards which indicate how many laps a skater has to complete in a race.

Pylons. The four corner-markers that mark the track the racers skate around.

Relay. A race between teams of skaters in which each relay team skater completes a portion of the race.

Equipment and Clothing

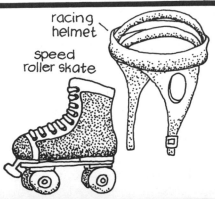

racing helmet

speed roller skate

Skates. Coaches prefer people to have their own skates in order to assure the best fit. Skates should fit snugly but not tightly. A little extra toe room is needed because your foot gets warmer and expands as you skate. The shoe of the skate should be cut

Roller-Skating Rink Operators Association of America

Two young racers.

high enough to provide ankle support. The wheels should be plastic. Skates with wooden or metal wheels are not allowed in competition. It's best to buy your skates at the rink or a store that specializes in athletic footwear. If you are not ready to buy skates, you can rent them at the roller rink.

Clothing. For your safety it is recommended that you wear a lightweight bike helmet. Roller skaters race in basketball-style shorts and long or short-sleeved team jerseys. Beginners sometimes wear tights underneath their shorts to protect against scrapes received in a fall.

What Makes a Good Racer

The key to successful racing is: getting off to a quick start, skillful skating around corners, and knowing how and when to pass your competitors.

Helpful Hints

From time to time, the shoes of your skates should be polished with saddle soap, and the dirty oil that builds up on the wheel bearings should be cleaned.

Use recreational rink time to practice skating. The more you skate the better racer you will become.

Bicycle riding and running will increase your stamina for this sport.

National speed skating championships are held once a year. To qualify you must participate in elimination events which are held throughout the country.

Where to Write for More Information

U.S. Amateur Confederation
of Roller Skating
P. O. Box 81846
Lincoln, Nebraska 68501

CHAPTER 6
Sports Camps: How to Choose One

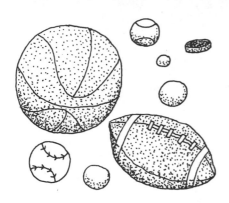

Sports camps can be a great help if you want to learn the basic skills of a game or if you want to improve what you already know. Camp sessions usually last one to two weeks and are either day or overnight camps. If you live near the camp, you may have the choice to sleep over or not. Camps for noncontact sports such as golf and tennis are usually coeducational. Camps that teach contact sports like football and ice hockey are held separately for girls and boys. Each camp is devoted to a single sport and usually provides special drills, individual and group instructions, competition, films, and guest appearances by noted sports personalities.

If you think you'd like to go to a sports camp, here are some things that might help you select one.

Find out what the camp will cost and exactly what you are paying for.

If you go to an outdoor camp, find out what indoor facilities are available. For example, if it is a tennis camp and indoor courts are limited, ask what the activities will be for rainy days.

Ask to see a schedule of a day's activities. Be sure there is at least three hours of instruction in the sport daily.

Find out how large the camp is and how many instructors there are for each camper.

If a celebrity athlete is associated with the camp, find out if he or she makes appearances and, if so, when. If the celebrity is scheduled during your session, find out how much time, if any, you can expect to spend with him or her.

How to Find Out about Sports Camps

Ask the coach in your school or someone in your

Faye Young (L. New York Stars) and Marcia Monk (R. Memphis State) instruct girls attending New York Stars Basketball Camp.

physical education program if he or she knows of any sports camps.

If your friends have gone to sports camps, ask them if they were satisfied with the instructions and facilities.

You may write to the following addresses and ask them to send you their lists of camps:

Advisory Council for Camps
400 Madison Avenue
New York, New York 10017

Women Sports Foundation
195 Moulton
San Francisco,
California 94123
(Send one dollar for a complete booklet of sports camps.)

CHAPTER 7
How to Be in the Game Without Playing

There are many sport-related jobs that can be had while you are still attending school. They may or may not pay wages but they will help you on the playing field. Some of them:

Assistant: Be a helping hand to a coach, trainer, or athletic director.

Bat Girl: For a professional baseball team.

Broadcaster: Try working with local radio and TV stations that cover your school's sporting events.

Caddy: At a local golf club or try shagging golf balls at a driving range.

Counselor: At a sports camp.

Manager: Help manage a team by taking care of equipment and supplies.

Official's Assistant: Help out at a game as a scorekeeper, timekeeper, or fieldmarker.

Photographer: Take photos of athletic events for newspapers and yearbook.

Pro's Assistant: Be a pro's extra hand—sweep or roll tennis courts at a local country club.

Referee: Help teachers by officiating at school games.

Reporter: Write about sports for your school paper.

Salesgirl: Work in a sporting goods department or store.

Usher: Ushering at sporting events.

In addition to the fun and self-satisfaction you can get from earning extra money as you work, if pay is involved, there are other good reasons for seeking out these jobs.

You might be able to use the facilities where you work— courts, rinks, and equipment.

You might be able to get free lessons.

You can improve your own game by watching others play.

You might learn a new sport.

How to Go After that Job

Don't be afraid to go to adults working in the sports field and ask if you can help them.

Most paying jobs are found through newspapers or bulletin boards at recreation centers. Also let your teachers, friends, and relatives know you want to work.

Look in the back of sports magazines for lists of job opportunities.

Write to professional or amateur teams in your area and ask about job possibilities.

Jobs in Your Future

When the time comes for you to go to work and you want to pursue a sports career, one way is to become a professional athlete. Another way is to work at jobs that are available both on and off the playing field. If you are interested in finding out more about these careers, write to the following addresses:

To find out about summer workshops for student athletic trainers, write to

Student Athletic
Trainer Workshop
Cramer Products Inc.
P. O. Box 1001
Gardner, Kansas 66030

Athletic Trainers
National Athletic
Trainers Assoc.
3315 South Street
Lafayette, Indiana 47904

Coaches
National Association for Girls
and Women in Sports
National Coaches Council
1201 16th Street N.W.
Washington, D.C. 20036

National High School Athletic
Coaches Assoc.
P. O. Box 16042
Orlando, Florida 32811

Community Recreation Workers
National Assoc. for Recreation
and Leisure
AAHPER
1201 16th Street N.W.
Washington, D.C. 20036

Officiating
N.A.G.W.S.
Affiliated Boards of Officials
1201 16th Street N.W.
Washington, D.C. 20005

Sports Medicine

American College of Sports Medicine
1440 Monroe Street
Madison, Wisconsin 53706

Public Relations

College Sports Information Directors of America
Princeton University
Princeton, New Jersey 08540

Business Managers

College Athletic Business Managers Association
University of Iowa
Iowa City, Iowa 52242

Sports Associations for Instruction and Information

Some places in your area that may offer instruction or the chance to play on a team are the local recreation departments, churches, YWCA, PAL, and scouting groups. You may also write to the following addresses for information and listings of competitive events:

American Alliance for Health, Physical Education and Recreation (AAHPER)
1201 16th Street N.W.
Washington, D.C. 20036

Women Sports Foundation
195 Moulton
San Francisco,
California 94123

Amateur Athletic Union of U.S.
3400 West 86th Street
Indianapolis, Indiana 46268
(sponsors the Junior Olympics)

Athletic Institute
Youth Sports Department
705 Merchandise Mart
Chicago, Illinois 60654

Exploring Program
Scouting U.S.A.
North Brunswick, New Jersey 08902

American Athletic Association for the Deaf
3916 Lantern Drive
Silver Spring, Maryland 20902

Blind Outdoor Leisure Development
533 East Main Street
Aspen, Colorado 81611

Special Olympics, Inc.
1701 K Street N.W.—Suite 203
Washington, D.C. 20006

President's Council on Physical Fitness
400 Sixth St. S.W.
Washington, D.C. 20201

Women's Sports Museum
Galveston, Indiana 46932

Glossary

Agility—Being able to move quickly and easily.

All-court Sneakers—Canvas shoes with rubber soles designed to be worn for a variety of sports.

Amateur—Playing a sport for recreation rather than as a profession.

Astroturf—A trademark for artificial grass used on playing fields.

Ball Control—To manipulate a ball while keeping control of it.

Block—To stop a ball or player.

Cleats—Studs of metal or plastic on the bottom of athletic shoes. Cleats provide traction for field sports.

Coach—A person who instructs and trains players in sports activities.

Conditioning—Getting into proper shape for a sport.

Contact Sport—A sport in which some physical contact with opposing players is part of the game.

Defense—The players who try to prevent the opponent from scoring.

Doubles—Racket sports competition in which two pairs of players compete against each other.

Foul—Breaking a rule in a game.

Goal—1. An area where the ball or puck must go in order to score. 2. A score made by getting a ball or puck into a goal.

Interference—Illegally hindering an opponent.

Little League—A national organization of baseball leagues in towns and cities for youngsters 8-12.

Noncontact Sport—A sport in which there is no physical contact allowed between players.

Offense—The players who try to score.

One-On-One—To play or practice against one other player.

Opponent—The team or individual played against in a game.

Playmaker—A player in a team sport who sets up offensive plays.

Professional—A person who makes a living in a sport.

Sprint—A short run at top speed.

Tie—When both sides in a game have the same scores.

Train—To prepare for competition.

Uniform—Clothing worn by team members to distinguish one team from another.

Violation—Generally used to mean the same as foul.

Index

Applebee, Constance, 41
Assistants jobs, 121
Athlete's foot, 19

Baggataway, 52
Baseball, 23-28; being a good
    player, 27-28; equipment,
    26-27; how to play, 26;
    information about, 28; little
    league, 23, 26, 28; players and
    terms, 24-26; where to play,
    23-24
Basketball, 8, 29-34; being a good
    player, 33-34; equipment, 33;
    how to play, 32-33; information
    about, 34; players and terms,
    30-32; where to play, 29
Bat girl, 121
Benefits of sports, 12-15
Bicycle road racing, 8, 15, 74-78;
    being a good racer, 77;
    equipment, 75-77; information
    about, 77-78; terms, 75; where
    and how to race, 75
Blanchard, Fessenden, 101
Blazejowski, Carol, 29, 33
Bleibtrey, Ethelda, 7
Blisters, 19-20
Bloody nose, 20
Boston Marathon, 9
Bowling, 15, 79-83; being a good
    bowler, 83; equipment, 82-83;
    how to bowl, 81; information
    about, 83; terms, 79-81; where
    to bowl, 79
Broadcaster, 121

Caddy, 121
Chapped lips, 17
Coaches, 122
Cogswell, James, 101
Counselor, 121
Currie, Cathie, 58

Dickenson, Amy, 23
Distance running, 9, 15, 84-88;
    being a good runner, 87-88;
    equipment, 85-87; information
    about, 88; terms, 85; where and
    how to run, 85

Ellis, William Webb, 46
Evert, Chris, 10
Exercise, 17
Eyes and eyeglasses, 17, 20

Fashion and sports, 8
Field hockey, 41-45; being a good
    player, 45; equipment, 44-45;
    how to play, 44; information
    about, 45; players and terms,
    41-44; where to play, 41
First aid, 19-21
Food and drink, 17-19
Football, 11, 46-51, 58; being a
    good player, 50-51; equipment,
    49-50; how to play, 49;
    information about, 51; players
    and terms, 47-49; where to play,
    47
Foster, Megan, 101

Glossary of terms, 125
Golf, 8, 89-94; being a good player,
    93-94; equipment, 92-93; how
    to play, 90-92; information
    about, 94; terms, 90; where to
    play, 89-90

Hamill, Dorothy, 10
Hancock, George, 63
Harpaston, 58
Henning, Anne, 110
Hockey; **See** Field hockey; Ice
    hockey
Holum, Diane, 110

126

Ice hockey, 11, 15, 35-40; being a good player, 39-40; equipment, 38; how to play, 37; information about, 40; players and terms, 35-37; where to play, 35
Ice skating (speed), 110-14; being a good racer, 112, 114; equipment, 111-12; information about, 114; terms, 111; where and how to skate, 110-11
Individual sports, 15, 73-118
Injuries, 19-21

Jefferson, Linda, 46
Joyce, Joan, 63

King, Billie Jean, 46, 95

Lacrosse, 52-57; being a good player, 56-57; equipment, 54-55; how to play, 54; information about, 57; players and terms, 53-54; where to play, 52-53

Manager, 120
Marathon, 9, 84
Mercatanti, Pat, 79
Merlin, Joseph, 115
Miller, Juliete, 68
Morgan, William, 68

Naismith, James, 29
Neuberger, Leah "Ping", 105

Ochowicz, Sheila Young, 110
Olympic games, 7, 10, 16, 29, 41, 110
Outerbridge, Mary, 95

Paganica, 89
Palmer, Sandra, 89

Photographer, 121
Ping-pong; **See** Table tennis
Platform tennis, 101-04; being a good player, 104; equipment, 103-04; how to play, 102; information about, 104; terms, 102; where to play, 101-02
Plimpton, J.L., 115

Racket sports, 15, 95-108; platform tennis, 101-04; table tennis, 105-08; tennis, 95-100
Reoch, Mary Jane, 74
Roller skating (speed), 115-18; being a good racer, 118; equipment, 117-18; information about, 118; terms, 116; where and how to race, 116
Row, Caroline, 115
Rudolph, Wilma, 10
Rugby, 46
Running; **See** Distance Running

Soccer, 46, 58-62; being a good player, 62; equipment, 60-62; how to play, 60; information about, 62; players and terms, 58-60; where to play, 58
Softball, 63-67; being a good player, 66-67; equipment, 65-66; how to play, 65; information about, 67; players and terms, 64-65; where to play, 63-64
Speed ice-skating; **See** Ice skating (speed)
Speed roller-skating; **See** Roller skating (speed)
Sports associations, 124
Sports camps, 119-20
Sports related jobs, 121-23
Stamm, Laura, 35
Sunburn, 20

Switzer, Katherine, 9, 84

Table tennis, 105-08; being a good player, 108; equipment, 108; how to play, 106-08; information about, 108; terms, 106; where to play, 105-06
Tammaro, Angela, 52
Team sports, 15, 22-72
Tennis, 8, 95-100; being a good player, 99-100; equipment, 99; how to play, 98; information about, 100; terms, 96-98; where to play, 95-96; **See also** Platform tennis; Table tennis
Trainers, 122

Usher, 121-22

Volleyball, 68-72; being a good player, 70-72; equipment, 70; how to play, 69-70; information about, 72; players and terms, 68-69; where to play, 68

Water, importance of, 18
Weather, 17
Wills, Helen, 95
Wingfield, Walter, 95
Womenand sports, history, 7-9; individual sports, 73-118; keeping in shape, 17-21; participation, 10-16; team sports, 22-72